THE OLD ENGLISH SHEEPDOG

POPULAR DOGS' BREED SERIES

THE OLD ENGLISH SHEEPDOG

ANN DAVIS

POPULAR DOGS
London Melbourne Auckland Johannesburg

Popular Dogs Publishing Co. Ltd.

An imprint of Century Hutchinson Ltd

Brookmount House, 62–65 Chandos Place,
London WC2N 4NW

Century Hutchinson Publishing Group (Australia) Pty Ltd
16–22 Church Street, Hawthorn, Melbourne, Victoria 3122

Century Hutchinson Group (NZ) Ltd
32–34 View Road, PO Box 40-086, Glenfield, Auckland 10

Century Hutchinson Group (SA) Pty Ltd
PO Box 337, Bergvlei 2012, South Africa

First published 1973
Second edition revised 1974
Third edition revised 1977
Fourth edition revised 1978
Fifth edition revised 1981
Sixth edition revised 1986

Set in Baskerville by BookEns, Saffron Walden, Essex

Printed and bound in Great Britain by Anchor Brendon Ltd,
Tiptree, Essex

ISBN 0 09 158130 3

CONTENTS

ACKNOWLEDGEMENTS

My very sincere thanks are due to the following, without whose help, encouragement, and understanding this book would never have been written:

The secretaries of the Kennel Club and the American Kennel Club for permission to reproduce their Breed Standards of the Old English Sheepdog. Further thanks are due to Commander J. S. Williams, to Mrs Chiverton, and to the staff of the Kennel Club in London for help in confirming certain facts and for allowing me access to the Kennel Club Library.

The following stalwarts of the breed kindly shared their memories of days gone by: Mrs M. Murray, Mrs M. Gibson, the late Mrs Ivy Cooke, the Misses Smailes and Knight-Bruce, Mrs Mary Bloor, Mrs Hilary Booth, Mrs Ellen Goodwin, Mr H. S. A. Smith, Mr Jim Rickard and Mr John Wasley.

From abroad I have been helped by: Dr Hugh Jordan and Mr John Mandeville (researcher extraordinaire) from America; Mrs Beatrice Ahonius from Finland; Mrs H. M. F. E. Backx-Benninck from Holland; Mrs Yvonne Mewis De Ryck from Belgium; Miss Judy Chapman and Mr Jim Hull from Australia; and many Scandinavian friends.

I am also grateful to my good friend Angela Mulliner for her extremely clear drawings which took many hours out of her already crowded life; to Mr and Mrs David J. Allison for their unstinting help and advice on the veterinary section; and to Florence Tilley for allowing me to peruse the Shepton records and press cuttings and for her assistance in tracing various facts.

There are many more who helped in varied ways, especially in submitting valuable photographs, who cannot be named owing to lack of space but to whom I will forever be indebted. Last, but not least, my gratitude goes to my family for all their help and encouragement.

A.D.

ILLUSTRATIONS

12   ILLUSTRATIONS

Ch Reculver Sugar Bush
Bred and owned by Mr and Mrs A. G. Wilkinson

Pastelblue Precious Maid
Bred by Lt-Col M. D. Lister
Owned by Mrs L. M. Back

Ch Beckington Lady of Welbyhouse
Bred by Messrs H. and R. Houghton
Owned by Mrs M. Gibson

Ch Prospect Shaggy Boy
Bred by Mrs Lawson
Owned by Mr Caj Haakansson

Ch Rollingsea Ringleader and Ch Wrightway's Glorious Day
Ringleader bred by Mrs J. Gould
Glorious Day bred by Mr and Mrs S. Fisher
Both owned by Mr and Mrs S. Fisher

Ch Keyingham Double Daisy
Bred and owned by Mrs M. Park

Ch Fernville Special Style of Trushayp
Bred by Mr N. W. R. Harrison
Owned by Mr and Mrs M. Lewis

Between pages 96 and 97

First feed

Body shape revealed by clipping

Ch Oakhill Peter Pan
Bred by Mrs M. Hargreaves
Owned by Mr and Mrs R. Ashcroft

Ch Pendlefold Prince Hal
Bred by Mr C. Riddiough
Owned by Mr and Mrs C. Riddiough

Ch Pendlefold Sweet Charity of Cinderwood
Bred by Mr C. Riddiough
Owned by Messrs M. Banks and H. Bentley

Bobbie Blue
Bred and owned by Mr Tom Cass

IN THE TEXT

Author's Introduction

When Popular Dogs approached me, in the early 1970s, with a view to publishing a comprehensive book on the Old English Sheepdog, it was with some hesitation that I agreed to write it. However, foresight was rewarded, for we have now seen several editions. With increased demand for the breed, it was inevitable that others would also write on the same subject, but over the past decade I have been encouraged by the continued interest, and correspondence received from both home and abroad. In this latest edition, the content has been slightly increased, more photographs added, and the Appendices have been up-dated to the end of December 1985.
1986   A.D.

1

Origins and Early History

IN *The Book of the Dog*, edited by Brian Vesey-Fitzgerald, there is a chapter on Old English Sheepdogs by A. S. L. Wallis, who refers to the theory that Columella wrote about the breed in what was possibly the 'first-ever' book on dogs. Although Mr Wallis cannot find anything in the text to suggest that Columella had this particular dog in mind, he does claim that the breed goes back to the fifteenth century at least, since both Van Eyck and Dürer have left portraits of a dog bearing a strong resemblance to the present-day Bobtail.

Another early writer who is often quoted is George-Louis Leclerc, Count de Buffon (1707–88). He wrote 'Of the 37 varieties, or races, of dogs given in the genealogical table, seventeen ought to be ascribed to the influence of climate. Group One consists of – The Shepherd's Dog, Spaniel, Siberian Dog, Mastiff, Harrier, Irish Greyhound, Gt. Danish Dog, Small, Spanish Dog, Bull Dog, The Pomeranian Dog, Iceland Dog, Lapland Dog, Common Greyhound, Hound, Terrier, Water Dog, and Turkish Dog.' He places all these breeds in one group because there is a much stronger and more obvious resemblance between them than between any other kinds; also because they all have sharp muzzles like the fox, erect ears, and an instinct for the protection of flocks. These are points which we immediately recognize, while others are described in the next part of his writings, where he states 'that the same race of dogs shall, in different climates, be totally changed from the appearance of the original stock in only two generations'.

His reasoning is as follows: 'The Shepherd's Dog, called the root of the tree, and this dog when transported to Lapland, or very cold climates, assumes an ugly appearance, and is contracted, by the effect of the frigid atmosphere, to a much smaller size; but in Russia, Iceland, and Siberia, where the climate is less rigorous, and the people some shades nearer civilisation, the same kind of dog is better accommodated and less changed.' He continues: 'These changes are occasioned solely by the influence of those climates, which produce no great alteration in the figure of the dog; for, in each of these climates, his ears are erect, his hair thick and long; his aspect wild; and he barks less frequently, and in a different manner, than in more favourable climates where he acquires a finer polish.'

Pursuing this argument, Count Buffon further comments that 'The same Shepherd's dog, when brought into temperate climates, and among a people perfectly civilised, as Britain, France and Germany, would, by a mere influence of climate, lose his savage aspect, his erect ears, his rude thick long hair, and assume the figure of a bull dog, the hound, or the Irish greyhound. . . . The hound is evidently the farthest removed, in similitude, from the Shepherd's dog; for his ears are long, soft, and entirely pendulous. The gentleness, docility and subservient timidity of the hound, are sufficient proof (if descended from the Shepherd's dog) of the wonderful perfection he has acquired by the long and careful education bestowed upon him by his protector, man.'

According to the tenets of Buffon, and those who have copied his writings and echoed his opinions, a description of this animal should have preceded every other of the canine race, as they maintain that every other branch (of whatever kind and propensity) has progressively sprung from this origin. This argument, however, is based mainly on conjecture, and there is little to support it except perhaps Buffon's rather vague disquisition upon 'the changes produced by the difference of climate'. These comments of Buffon and his contemporaries were reproduced in *The Sportsman's Cabinet* and later quoted: 'It is most probable, that for a great length of time, in the earliest ages, the protection of the flock and the

preservation of domestic animals were the only purposes to
which the dog became appropriate; from which circumstances
alone it has been erroneously supposed, that the Shepherds or
sheep dog was the first, or parent stock from which every other
has been produced.' Used to illustrate this chapter in *The
Sportsman's Cabinet*, was the very famous picture called 'The
Shepherd's Dog' by Reinagle. This is perhaps a suitable point
to mention that although early writings refer to the Shepherd's
Dog, they became more familiarly known as Sheep Dogs in
every rural district of the country.

Another writer was Juliana Barnes, a Mother Superior (born
1388). In her *Boke of St. Albans*, she notes that dogs in Roman
times were divided into six classes, one of which was Shepherd
Dogs (*Canes Pastorales Pecuarii*) and comments, 'The Shepherd
dog was often provided with a spiked collar round its neck, as a
protection against wolves.' In 1578 Abraham Fleming listed
'The Shepherd's Dogge' amongst *British Dogs*, but says only
that '*Canis Domesticus* has erect ears and the tail is woolly underneath'. Bewick, in 1790, spoke of 'the Shepherd's Dog – a typical
collie'. In a book published in 1904, Herbert Compton quotes
Barnaby Googe's translation of Conrad Heresbatch's *Foure
Books of Husbandrie* (published in 1586) in which the 'ideal' Old
English Sheepdog of that period is described 'The Shepherd's
masty, that is for the folde, must neither be so gaunt nor so
swifte as the greyhound, nor so fatte nor so heavy as the masty
of the house, but verie strong and able to fighte and follow the
chase, that he may beat away the woolfe or other beasts, and to
follow the theefe, and to recover the prey. And therefore his
body should be rather long than short and thick; in all other
points he must agree with the ban-dog. His head must be great
and smooth and full of veins, his ears great and hanging; his
joints long; his forelegs shorter than his hinder; but verie
straight and great. His claws wide, nails hard, his heel neither
fleshy nor too hard; the ridge of his back not too much
appearing, nor crooked; his ribs round and well-knitte; his
shoulder points well distant; his buttocks fatte and broad.' The
picturesque wording alone seems well worth reading.

A book published in 1844 describes the Old English Sheepdog: 'Whilst the Collie is the Scottish and Welsh Sheepdog, the present animal is the original, or true, English one. It is larger and less shaggy than the Collie. In some individuals the ears are erect, and others have the tail very short – the latter peculiarity being apparently inherited from parents whose tails have been cut.'* *Dogs of the British Islands*, edited by Stonehenge in 1872, has a heading 'Sheep and Drover Dogs', wherein the English Sheepdog is quoted: '. . . whether rough or smooth, is to be found in various colours. It is a common thing to see them grizzle, black, red, brindled, or (for the most part) white; and we have also observed a dull rust colour, patched with black, in the smooth dog. This variety has frequently what are called "china" or "walled eyes". As the Shepherd's dog under old excise laws was only exempt from tax when the tail was cut off, it was formerly always removed, and in process of time many mothers produced litters – or parts of litters – wholly without tails, and an instance of this has occurred in our own experience.'(!)

Returning to *The Sportsman's Cabinet*, we read that 'This dog is the most timid, obedient, placid, serene, and grateful in creation; he seems studiously conscious of the purposes for which he was formed, and is never so perceptibly gratified as when affording the most incessant proof of his unsullied integrity. Instinctively prone to industry, he is alive to the slightest sensation of his employer . . .' Later we read that 'The breed is propagated and preserved with the greatest respect to purity in the Northern parts of the Kingdom, as well as in the Highlands of Scotland, where in the extensive tracts and uncultivated wilds their services exceed description.' He is then praised for his knowledge of which sheep belong to his particular flock, and his ability to weed out intruders, particularly noticeable in the downy hills of Hampshire and Wiltshire.

The Sheepdog was not only described as a worker, but also as a life-saver. It seems that in the year 1796 Mr Henry Hawkes, a farmer, of Halling in Kent, was returning late from Maidstone Market, rather the worse for drink. After stopping at Aylesford for more drink, he was even more inebriated as he

---

* They certainly did not know much about genetics in those days.

continued on his way. He passed through the village of Newhead safely, and then fell into deep snow near Snodland Brook. Completely overcome by drink or sleep (or both), he would have perished in the extreme cold had it not been for his faithful sheepdog who 'mounted upon the exposed body, rolled himself round, and "laid" down upon his master's bosom, for which his shaggy coat proved a most seasonable covering, and eventual protection during the dreadful severity of the night, the snow falling all the time.' The next morning, someone out with a gun saw what appeared to be some kind of fowl on the frozen ground, but at his approach the dog disentangled itself from the encrustation of snow and encouraged him to come nearer the recumbent figure of his master. The almost lifeless farmer was soon taken to a nearby house where he quickly recovered. In his gratitude, the farmer ordered a silver collar to be made for the dog, and later turned down an offer from a wealthy gentleman in the neighbourhood who wanted to buy the dog for what was then the enormous sum of ten guineas.

Idstone, in 1883, writes of one class of Sheepdog in Oxon, Wilts, Berks, Hants and Dorset, which he regards as the typical English Sheepdog. 'Blue, grizzled, rough-haired, large-limbed, surly, small-eared, small-eyed, leggy, bob-tailed dog' is the description he gives, and he also mentions that 'He will, though such dogs are rare, run over the backs of the flock, to head them in a lane.'

While the foregoing makes interesting reading, there is no clear explanation as to how the Old English Sheepdog evolved, and no indication that it resulted from the crossing of a couple or more breeds; it seems that Bobtails, like Topsy, 'just growed'. Many writers over the years have attempted to trace their origins, and one theory seems to be that they were descended from the Russian Owtchah. Indeed, as far back as 1910 we read in the *Kennel Encyclopaedia* (edited by J. Sidney Turner) that the Russian Owtchah was the most closely approximate, the main differences being its greater size and a well-feathered tail. He goes on to say, 'Many authorities believe that it is from this parent stock that the English Sheepdog and Scotch Bearded Collie have their origin, and that the fierceness necessary for the protection of their charges from the attacks of wild animals has given place to a smaller and better-tempered animal in our more peaceful times and country.'

Besides being linked with the Russian dog, the Bobtail has been likened to the Berger du Brie, while the shape is not unlike that of the Komondor. Various writers have mentioned the particular type of herding collie dog that was common in their particular part of the country, and we have heard of the Sussex type which was used mostly for driving both cattle and horses in to market. With the coming of the railways, these dogs lost their use and the numbers dwindled. It does seem that today's glamorous Sheepdogs may well have developed from the very selective breeding of the stock that proved itself of good appearance and able to move at a pace when required. The drovers' dogs were sometimes called the Smithfield Collie, as it was to this famous market that they herded the cattle and sheep.

In a book published in 1907, there is reference to a police sergeant at Kirkham who had been given what was called a Russian Terrier. It was described as being no terrier, but to all intents and purposes a fine sheepdog, with the tail left untouched. His shape is depicted as 'big and blocky, with massive bone, and full, correct coat, of white with merle markings. Strong, active, and good natured, in general conduct staid and dignified.' This dog is said to have been received as a gift around the year 1857, and to anyone reading the full description it cannot fail to appear as a Bobtail-like figure. So many writers refer to what seem to be Bobtails; they vary in matters of detail, but all agree on the shaggy appearance. One book notes that plenty of fresh air is essential if the harsh coat is to be kept, plus ample supplies of fresh water. A weatherproof kennel free from draughts is enough, and it is stated that the dog does best on bare, wooden boards. 'He hates to be chained up, which spoils his temper, and cramps his action. If he can run loose, and take unlimited exercise, he is in his element.' This book adds that he is an excellent sporting dog, making an admirable retriever, being light-mouthed and fond of water, keen of scent, and fast enough to pick up a wounded hare or rabbit.

In 1845 W. C. L. Martin wrote, 'Let us now turn to the shepherds dog of our own islands, and the adjacent parts of the Continent, which offer several varieties, more or less different from each other. One breed from the North is covered with a deep woolly coat, capable of felting; another breed that is generally depicted is covered with long flowing hair, and the tail is full of brushes; the colour is generally black, with tanned limbs and muzzle, varied occasionally with white on the breast. In both, the muzzle is acute and the ears erect or nearly so. There is a third and larger breed, called the drovers dog. This last dog generally had short hair, but some had the woolly coat.'

Bobtails have been painted many times over the years, and the most famous and often reproduced shows the Duke of Buccleuch (with recognizable dog) painted in 1771 by Gainsborough. Another popular pictorial record is called 'The Shepherd's Dog' by Philip Reinagle, and as mentioned earlier in this chapter it was used to illustrate *The Sportsman's Cabinet* and published in 1803. In 1835, the artist Sidney Cooper painted an Old English Sheepdog, and this was blue and white, big-boned in head and body.

Eventually the breed became sufficiently popular to be scheduled at dog shows, and at the Curzon Hall in Birmingham in 1873 there were three exhibitors. The judge, Mr M. B. Wynn, awarded only a second prize because he found the quality so poor. This small entry and lack of quality could have put an end to the Bobtail as a show dog, but fortunately in 1889 Mr Freeman-Lloyd produced an interesting pamphlet on the breed; this must have aroused some interest, for the Old English Sheepdog Club had been founded the previous year (1888), there being quite a few owners by then.

There were several pioneer owners and breeders in the early days: Dr Edwardes-Ker was not only a practical owner but also clever with his pen, and not above writing very 'down-to-earth' comments if he thought fit. The first President of the Old English Sheepdog Club, Sir Humphrey de Trafford, held that office from the formation of the Club until 1911, when it was decided that in future Presidents should be elected annually. He was followed by Mr H. Dickson, and then Mr W. G. Weager. The Club's first lady President was Mrs Fare Fosse, who was to go down in history as the owner of Ch Fairweather; this bitch became very well known in years to come, for when she died her body was given to the taxidermist and can be seen to this day as part of a special canine exhibition at the country annexe to the Natural History Museum at Tring. Mr Parry Thomas was one of the early enthusiasts from Wales who bred some very sound stock. Dr W. Bott has also been named as a clever breeder and judge, who helped to prevent the breed from becoming too large, insisting on both type and quality; he was the owner of Ch Bouncer.

Another dog worth mentioning is Dr Locke's Ch Sir Cavendish, bred by Dr Edwardes-Ker in May 1887; sired by Caradoc, out of Dame Ruth, he won at Liverpool, Manchester, Birmingham, Bath, Leeds, Cruft's and Crystal Palace in 1890, 1891 and 1892. Also listed are Dr Bott's Ch Bouncer, Dr MacGill's Ch Watch Boy, Sir Humphrey de Trafford's Ch Dame Barbara, and Mr H. Dickson's Harkaway and Ch Lady Scaramouche. Ch Handsome Boy, whose parentage is given as sired by Stylish Box out of Dolly Daydream, bred by Mrs F. Travis, was born in July 1902 and sold to Dr Dickson who later sold him to an American owner. In England he won CCs at Cheltenham, Blackpool, Southampton (2), Richmond, Bristol, Crystal Palace and Birmingham, where he won the Lord Mayor's Cup and the Breeders' 25 guineas Cup for the Best Collie or Sheep Dog in the Show. Mr Weager's Ch Dairymaid, Mr Clayton's Ch Victor Cavendish, Mr Wilmot's Ch Robert the Bobby and Sergeant Bruce were also well known. Mrs Fare Fosse is probably best remembered as breeder of the famous bitch Ch Fairweather; born in 1898 by Sir James out of Birthday, she won some 20 CCs during her career. However, she also owned Wall-Eyed Bob, whose parentage is unknown; he was probably born about 1885, and won well up to the time of his death in 1898.

Also to be remembered are Mrs Rivers, who owned the well-

known winners Ch Ragged Man and Hampshire Lad, and Mrs
Runciman who goes down in history as owner of Ch Beat the
Band. Mrs Charters' famous Ch Brentwood Country Girl is
recorded as being by Roseberry, out of Queen Maisie; bred by
Dr Dickson in September 1902, she won 12 CCs and 13
Reserve CCs in four years, besides Cups and Specials for Best
Bitch in Show, and more than 200 other prizes.

Undoubtedly, the most famous Old English Sheepdog
kennels in the world are those at Shepton Mallet, belonging to
the Tilley family. They first belonged to W. T. S. Tilley, who
also made a name for himself in the West Country as a prize-
winning wine-maker (his cider gained many awards), while his
wife produced prize-winning cheeses. He built up the Shepton
Kennels with his brother, H. A. Tilley, to whom they passed on
his death. When H. A. Tilley died, the kennels went to his
daughter, Miss Florence Tilley who died in June 1985. The
Shepton Kennels have produced too many famous winners to
list in full, but in the early days such Champions as Bouncing
Lass, Dolly Gray and Shepton Laddie were amongst the best
known. Ch Bouncing Lass was bred by Mr E. Y. Butterworth in
June 1899; her sire was Young Watch, and her dam Peggy
Primrose. She won about a dozen CCs and secured special
prizes as the Best Exhibit in any breed at eleven different
shows; she was sold to America in 1903. Ch Dolly Gray was
born in April 1901, and bred by Mrs F. Travis; she is stated to
have been 'own sister' to Ch Handsome Boy, so one presumes
that this is equivalent to our 'litter-sister'. Their sire was Stylish
Boy, and the dam was Dolly Daydream. In four years Dolly
Gray won twelve CCs, 130 first prizes, 300 Specials, and had
nine Best-in-shows to her credit.

Mr Tilley founded the Old English Sheepdog Club of
America in 1904, and crossed the Atlantic many times to show
his dogs at the big events over there. Bouncing Lass became an
International Champion, making the return journey to
America no less than three times. Although the Old English
Sheepdog Club in this country was founded in 1888 by only
half-a-dozen enthusiasts, they gradually attracted more mem-
bers and in 1910 the membership was between seventy and

eighty. In 1894 they held their own show, and in 1899 it is recorded that at many South Country shows several classes were provided for Bobtails which attracted good entries. At the Kennel Club Show there were fifty entries, whilst at a smaller event held at Streatham there were forty-six. The Old English Sheepdog Club held an Annual Show each spring in conjunction with the Collie Club, when valuable cups, medals and specials were competed for; they also had Breeders Produce Stakes which were well supported. In addition the Club offered Special Prizes and Silver Medals for competition at all the leading shows. Well-known breeders and exhibitors at this time included Miss Acton, Mrs Brigham, Miss Davidson, Mrs Mayhew, Mrs Monkton, Mrs Jocelyn Otway and Miss Wild, also Captain Falls, Mr Freeman Lloyd, Mr Macbeth, Mr T. H. Short, Mr Parry Thomas, Mr P. Ullman and Mr S. Woodiwiss.

Aubrey Hopwood wrote an excellent book on the breed, and if anyone is fortunate enough to own a copy nowadays then they have a possession greatly to be prized. Copies have been sold for sizeable sums, and I know of one American who would pay almost anything to acquire his own copy. Hopwood wrote in the halcyon days when the spirit of sportsmanship was abundant, and there were many people in a sound financial position who could enjoy all their canine pursuits with no worry about possible financial returns. Life must have been enormous fun – competition was as keen as it is now, but from old accounts it seems that no one minded whether they won or lost as long as the company had been pleasant and the judging fair. Over half a century ago writers were much more forthright than they are today, and if one of them thought that a judge was not on the level, he did not hesitate to say so!

In addition to his own book on the breed, Aubrey Hopwood was frequently persuaded to contribute to works encompassing all breeds of dogs, and some of his writings can be easily interpreted to apply to present-day circumstances. In one volume he states, 'With regard to the present type, there is very little fault to be found, and it is probable that there is, at this moment, a larger proportion of good all-round Bobtails in

England than at any other previous period in the breed's history. Also, there is undoubtedly a greater unanimity of opinion as to correctness of type and character. A craze for out-sized dogs has died a natural death, and it is to be hoped that a foolish practice of exhibiting Bobtails with their coats full of white powder will speedily follow suit. The weakest point at present is the texture of coat, which is very rarely harsh enough, and has in many instances, a decided tendency to softness and woolliness, which should be strenuously guarded against. A lack of strength and squareness in jaw and fore-face is also occasionally observable, and the combination of these two failings is the greatest danger which now threatens the character of the breed. With these two reservations, the Old English Sheepdog of today is as good as ever he was, and taking into consideration the enormous increase in his numbers, the average standard of merit is unusually well maintained.' When one considers that this was written in 1910, one wonders whether Aubrey Hopwood would say the same about present-day Bobtails!

Some of his earlier writings (1907) emphasize his intense dislike of the over-powdering of Bobtails in the show ring, and he also regrets the incidence of heavy shoulders, undue length of fore-face and snipiness of muzzle, which seemed to be on the increase at that time. He advised on the selection of studs as follows: 'When planning breedings, instead of running after a popular prize-winner regardless, they should strive to breed for results, and attempt to eradicate faults by judicious selection instead of aggravating them.' Good as he considered the breed at that time, he mentioned points that he thought could well be improved upon – compactness of body, shortness of back, clean shoulders, harshness of coat, strength of jaw and fore-face. He placed the onus on judges for the maintenance of quality!

We owe a great debt of gratitude to some of the stalwarts who owned Bobtails before the last war, and who managed to keep a few of them going through the dark days of air-raids, rationing and so on. Mrs Murray has told me the story of how they used to queue up for hours on end just to get a little food for the dog, and how glad they were to get hold of cow-udder. The late Mrs Ivy Cooke was another who recalled the days of food shortages, and how she managed to obtain some goat meat from a slaughterhouse. Towards the end of the war, I can remember a dog-meat shop quite near to us, which opened about twice a week to sell brightly-stained meat, fit only for animals. The number of 'hopefuls' waiting for one or two pounds of dog meat had to be seen to be believed; they started to queue about two hours before the shop opened, standing in an orderly line whatever the weather.

Even after the war there were food shortages, so it was not easy to increase the numbers of the breed very quickly. One dog who lived through the war was the great Ch Sir John Marksman, bred by Miss Irene Webster. Whelped on 26 February, he entered the show ring at the age of seven months, when at his first show he was placed first in both Puppy and Junior Classes. He was shown extensively under all the leading judges, and unbeaten until eighteen months old. Winner of over 200 first prizes, he gained his first CC in 1938 at Cruft's, when the judge was Miss Tireman (judge at the first Championship Show held by the Old English Sheepdog Club of Wales in 1971). His second CC was awarded by Mr H. A. Tilley at Kensington, and his qualifying CC at Harrogate under Mrs Gatehouse. The war cut short his show career, but he was usefully employed at stud and produced some outstanding progeny. This great dog died in his sleep on 30 January 1947, having had and given twelve good years. Many present-day pedigrees go back to his line – Showman of Pett, Pastelblue Sir John, Cheddar of Pastelblue were all well-known progeny, and Marco of Pastelblue – a son of Sir John – went to France. The breed is greatly indebted to folk of Miss Webster's calibre, for it is from their stock that so many of the present blood-lines come.

Miss Tireman, whose Pastorale Kennels figure in many pedigrees, still judges from time to time; she was the owner of the well-known Ch Tommy Tittlemouse. Mrs Sheffield is another who is still very active, frequently seen at Championship Shows. In addition to the Bobtails, she made her

Hillgarth prefix known in Whippets, so is the breeder of champions in both breeds.

Mrs Mabel Gibson (Cruft's Bobtail judge 1973), despite some ill-health, managed to put some superb examples into the show ring. I do not think anyone can better the grooming and presentation of her 'Beckington' Bobtails. Her Ch Stoneybroke was a well-known winner in the past, and her Tom Tod and Lady are referred to in greater detail later in this chapter.

Miss Tucker of the 'Watchers' Kennels bred her last litter in the early 1960s. Her last Bobtail died in the mid sixties but her bloodlines are still very evident in some pedigrees.

The Misses Smailes and Knight-Bruce were great enthusiasts, who had their first pedigree Bobtail from Miss Palmer, at one time Secretary and Treasurer, later President, of the Old English Sheepdog Club. This first dog was of the Tenet prefix, from Miss Palmer's fairly large kennel of Bobtails at Thanet. There were many sheep in this area, and she trained some of the dogs to herd them. The Misses Smailes and Knight-Bruce lived at one time near Miss Tireman, who owned Corydon of Pastorale; he was the sire of Boris of Bewkes, the first export from their kennel, the dam being Raggedy Ann of Bewkes. One of their dogs is still quite high in current pedigrees – Julian of Bewkes, who was mated to Ch Pastelblue Carol Ann; from this litter came some of the Reculver breeding that has spread into many pedigrees. Since those days, these two ladies bred and showed many good dogs, kept up their interest in the Old English Sheepdog, and were keen observers at the ringside when Bobtails were exhibited anywhere near their part of Dorset.

Following the war years, the breed maintained a very steady position for a long time, apart from occasional minor fluctuations. Then came the gradual rise in popularity, not only in the UK but elsewhere in the world. Some attribute this to the use of Bobtails in advertising, and we realize that the breed is recognized by virtue of its appearance when advertising a well-known British paint, and earlier, a brand of carpets. In America, the breed has enhanced the advertisements of a large motor manufacturer, also raincoats and so on, but I am not convinced that advertising accounts for a very high percentage of the increase in numbers. Pedigree dogs have become more popular generally, and the Bobtail, with its gentle ambling ways and superb temperament, cannot be bettered as a pet for the family, being an ideal companion for children of all ages and an excellent house guard. Our first Bobtail was the self-appointed nurse-cum-guard of our daughter, and he would station himself by her pram from early days, though he was only a young puppy. When still a puppy, he helped her with her first steps, patiently waiting while she pulled herself erect by grabbing hold of his coat and hauling herself up.

One advantage of Bobtails being seen more often in public is that prospective owners can see the differing types and quality, thus becoming more selective when it comes to acquiring a Bobtail for themselves. One of the early advertise-ments showing a Bobtail was when one of Mr Gooch's 'Farleydenes' was advertising a well-known brand of carpet, but the Old English Sheepdog was replaced by a cat after a time. The best-known, however, was the one already men-tioned for the famous brand of paint, posed over many years by Mr & Mrs Sharpe's Dash (correctly known as Shepton Daphnis Horsa). Having occupied the position of Dulux Dog for quite some time, he was retired with a great fanfare, and his successor elected by means of a national photographic com-petition attracting over 400 entries. The photos were all examined, and six finalists were selected. These dogs were brought up to the advertising agents in London, where they were carefully judged for various qualities, the final winner being Norman Harrison's late Ch Fernville Lord Digby. The breed has often been used in films too, and the Sharpes' Dash was no stranger to film studios. In America the Old English Sheepdog is also a film star, Lord Nelson being about the best known. *The Shaggy Dog, Summer Magic* and *Chitty Chitty Bang Bang* are successful films which come to mind, the first two being made in the United States, the latter in the United Kingdom. The latest UK film featuring a Bobtail was *Digby – The Biggest Dog in the World* which used Mrs Pat Creed's Mosshall Lady Joy early and late in the film, and Mr and Mrs Glass's Twotrees Brandysnap as the dog when he grew enormous through drinking a chemical.

With the rise in popularity, demand has pushed up the purchase price quite considerably, and one must also take into account the ever-rising cost of feeding, unavoidable increases in veterinary fees and so on. Our first Bobtail cost us just £16, but prices on this level are now out of date. Many years ago high prices were paid on isolated occasions for something extra special, and no doubt this will continue in the future. It is hard to anticipate what sort of prices are likely to be fetched by puppies in the next year or so, as there is no doubt that the demand is not so great as it was. There is a level below which it is not an economic proposition to breed a litter, so newcomers to the breed must expect to pay a fair price. If a Bobtail is to end up as a good sound specimen, it must be fed with the right food in correct quantities, and this must be borne in mind when costing out a litter. Other costs to take into account are the veterinary bills, stud fees and so on. A reliable breeder will take great care in the raising of a litter, and is entitled to expect to recoup his outgoings. What one does not anticipate is that the price of a puppy should be loaded with the costs of keeping all the other dogs in a fair-sized kennel!

It is hard for the present-day single-handed breeder to find that what was once a good pet market is being flooded with inferior quality stock, literally churned out on a puppy farm or similar establishment. I do not consider the breed lends itself to mass-production. A lot of temperament troubles in many breeds can probably be attributed to environmental dif-ficulties, for puppies need love and the attention which gives them a feeling of security, and this cannot be so when the owner is either out at work all day, or else the litter is one of many, none of which receive more attention than is absolutely essential. Fortunately we have been blessed through the years with breeders who carefully study all available blood-lines in an attempt to maintain, and if possible upgrade, the quality of the stock. They have the patience to run on what appears to be a promising puppy, and when they find that their hunch is correct they show it with care, so that later a super specimen may be used to future advantage by others in the breed. Equally conscientious are those who through unavoidable circumstances are never able to get their stock into the show ring, and facing this fact try to ensure that any animals showing promise will go to a home where there is every chance that they may be exhibited.

One breeder who realized a dog's potential, and made up her mind to let him go where he would be extensively shown, was Mrs Hilary Booth; the dog was International Ch Shepton Sonny Boy of Marlay. When she was leaving school in 1939, in Ireland, she was given his sire, registered as Beau Brigand of Marlay. Bred in Ireland from Shepton stock, he was trained to herd cattle and was also shown. When she joined the British Land Army in 1940, Mrs Booth had to leave her dog behind, but when she later married she was able to have him back. She later bought a sweet bitch from Miss Webster, called Comedy Starlight, who was – with her very 'typy' shape and lovely temperament – the ideal mate for Brigand, a very big, masculine dog. This was the foundation of the Marlay breeding.

A youngster kept from one of the litters was called Marlay Top Dog, but his name was later changed to Sonny Boy of Marlay. (Some years ago it was possible to change a dog's registered name at the Kennel Club.) He was shown, and won quite well, as a puppy, but Mrs Booth felt that she could not do him justice, so he went to Miss Tilley who added the Shepton prefix to his name. She won with him, and he was later sold to Mrs Jones, winning seventeen CCs in all. His parents were great favourites during the war with the children, from whom they collected pennies in their special boxes for the Red Cross, raising over £200 in this way. They were with Mrs Booth when they went through the dreadful May blitz on Liverpool, when it was possible to read a newspaper at midnight by the light of the flames from the burning buildings. After this, they suffered from gun-shyness as a result of the noise from a huge mobile gun that was parked on a temporary gun site at the farm.

Another Bobtail who was a good winner was Ch Shepton Indomitable; although he did not sire so many litters, his name often crops up in pedigrees and he was the winner of no less than nineteen CCs. He was the son of Champion parents, going back through his sire Ch Shepton Surf King to Mrs Grillett's Boldwood breeding; his parents were Boldwood Bombardier and Boldwood Bustle, his dam being of Mrs Shanks's breeding out of Snow White of Pickhurst by the very well-known Nosey Parker of Pickhurst. Mrs Gibson's home-bred Ch Beckington Tom Tod, son of Shepton Celebrity and Shepton Charming, is another to keep in mind; he amassed some fifteen CCs. Holding the record for a number of years for the greatest number of CCs won in the breed was Mrs Gibson's other famous Bobtail, Ch Beckington Lady of Welbyhouse; daughter of Shepton Bridewell Brave Brigadier, she was out of Shepton Butterfly, bred by H. & R. Houghton, and in her show-life accounted for no less than twenty-nine CCs.

In more recent times, Mrs Edna Foster's Ch Bevere Proud Monarch won fifteen CCs. Close behind is Mrs Jean Gould's Ch Rollingsea Snowboots, winner of eighteen CCs. Never a champion, but to his owner surely 'the greatest', was Mrs Woodford's late Baucottblues Boy, sire in this country of no less than five Champions, plus others overseas.

Mr & Mrs Ashcroft's Ch Oakhill Peter Pan can claim a special place in breed history as the sire of Mr & Mrs Riddiough's Ch Pendlefold Prince Hal, whom they bred themselves in their very first litter. He was the top winner in 1970 and 1971, and had to his credit two Supreme Bests in Show at Championship Shows, one at Three Counties in June 1970, and the other at Windsor in 1971. He was also a multiple Group winner, and has had many Bests of Breed at both Open and Championship Shows. At the time of his death, he had a total of thirty-three CCs, and had beaten the all-time record earlier mentioned as being held by Ch Beckington Lady of Welbyhouse. His sister, from a later litter, took her title at the last Championship Show of 1971 – Ch Pendlefold Sweet Charity of Cinderwood.

Norman Harrison's Ch Fernville Fernando, although winning only four CCs, nevertheless made his mark on the breed as a sire, accounting in this country for his daughter, Ch Fernville Fantasy, who made breed history by getting the triple at Cruft's – CCs in 1963, 1964, and 1965. He was also the sire of Mrs Gibson's Ch Beckington Fernville Flamingo, winner of eight CCs, and of Mr and Mrs Smith's Fernville Flanagan, winner of three CCs. Mr & Mrs Westwell's Ch Sukray Statesman was another son, winner of four CCs. Abroad, especially in America, Fernando has been hailed as the sire of much good stock, with Champion progeny to prove it. Another Champion sire with Champion offspring was International Ch Shepton Sonny Boy of Marlay, with six Champion progeny to his credit.

In recent times, Old English Sheepdogs have made their mark in both the Group and BIS ring, with Ch Lameda Perfect Pal going Supreme BIS at LKA 1974. Ch Fernville Special Style of Trushayp took BIS at both Windsor and LKA in 1975. Ch Aberfells Georgy Porgy, who held the title of top winner of all time from 1979 to 1984, was the winner of 36 CCs, nine Groups and Supreme BIS at Leeds 1977, and WELKS and LKA in 1978. One of his sons, Ch Cinderwood Great Gatsby of Bartine, was a Group winner also, with Supreme BIS at Border Union 1978 to his credit. Ch Keyingham Double Daisy, also a Group winner, went through to Supreme BIS at Bournemouth in 1979 and was that year's top winner in the breed, not an easy achievement for a bitch.

The current top winner is Ch Jedforest Don Carlos, who had 39 CCs to his credit at the end of 1984, with nine Groups and Supreme BIS at SKC 1983, as well as being top winner in the breed for the years 1982–83 and 1984. Carlos was retired from competition upon winning his fortieth CC, and BOB, at the Southern Counties Championship Show on 2 June 1985.

1985 high flyer was Ch Barnolby Troubleshooter of Oldoak, who went Best in Show at Paignton Championship Show. Another to hit the top spot was Ch Pelajilo Dan Dare, who went Best in Show at the Working Breeds of Scotland Championship Show.

(Sally Anne Thompson)

Ch Reculver Christopher Robin

(Sally Anne Thompson)

Ch Reculver Little Rascal

Old English Sheepdog, *c.* 1910. Oil painting by Lilian Cheviot

Ch Moonshine Weather

Ch Tommy Tittle-
mouse of Pastorale
(*Thomas Fall*)

Ch Highroad
Robbery
(*Thomas Fall*)

(*Thomas Fall*)
Ch Pastorale Mistress of Fulson, Master Courtesy of Fulson,
Pastorale Dame of Fulson

(*Thomas Fall*)

Ch Bashurst Sally Ann of Pickhurst

(*Thomas Fall*)

Boldwood Berengaria

2

The Breed Standard

THE meeting of the World Kennel Clubs, held some little while ago, discussed in great detail the subject of unification of breed standards. It was agreed by delegates present that they would, on return to their respective countries, set in motion the processes to put their standards into a universally acceptable format. To my knowledge, the only country to do exactly as planned was the United Kingdom! There was not, and has not been since, any intention to CHANGE breed standards. It had been agreed that such a mammoth task would enable certain clarifications to be made, plus any omissions which had become evident through the years to be rectified. In all its dealings with the Breed Clubs concerned, the British Kennel Club has made it abundantly plain that it was not seeking to re-design breeds! The new format was to be in the order in which judges would appraise the animal, thus starting with General Appearance, Characteristics and Temperament before going into Conformation.

Sadly, the rabble-rousers saw fit to stir up dissent throughout the dog-owning world, and the Kennel Club, Breed Clubs, and individuals were subjected to harassment over what should have been an essential and friendly exercise. After all, if quality is to be maintained, then it is in everyone's interest that the breed standard should be as helpful as possible on all points. Through the years, we are well aware that the older, experienced breeders had in mind certain priorities when either selecting stock or adjudging quality in the centre of the show ring. Too many of these essential breed points were carried in the head, told to listeners, but had not been written

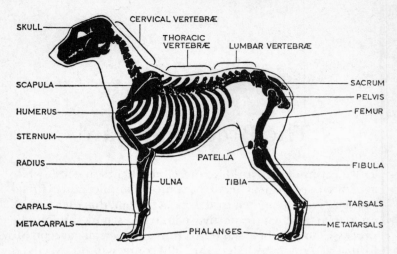

Figure 1   Skeleton of the Old English Sheepdog

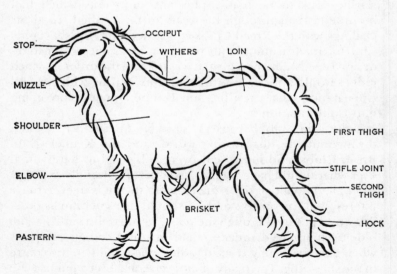

Figure 2   Points of the Old English Sheepdog

down for all to see. Our OES Standard did not have sections on characteristics and temperament, and the brief mention of pigmentation was merely that the nose should be large, BLACK and capacious – no mention of pigment around the eyes or lips! Obviously, there were things which did need clarification, and so following the Kennel Club's letter of December 1982 to all the registered Breed Clubs, the parent club (The OES Club) contacted the other ten clubs to suggest that they consider a joint meeting, at which we could iron out any problems, and thus put a united reply to the Kennel Club. The regional clubs dealt with the Standard in various ways,

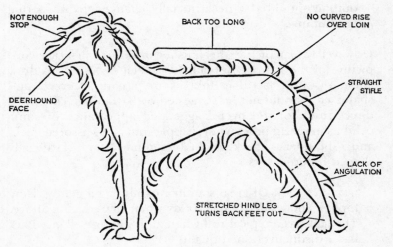

Figure 3   Faults

and were then able to come to the joint meeting well briefed to speak and vote on behalf of their memberships. Ten clubs were represented, with notes from the one absentee (Northern Ireland) which were introduced during discussion. Of those persons attending, eighteen are now approved by the Kennel Club to award Challenge Certificates. Full and frank discussion took place, with voting on any contended points. Suffice to say that anything on which queries were raised was passed by large majorities. The results of the day's efforts were circulated to the clubs for their approval and then submitted to the Kennel Club. With but minor editing, the Kennel Club's Breed Standards Committee accepted the Joint Clubs' submission, which is most gratifying.

1986 British Kennel Club Standard

General Appearance Strong, square-looking dog of great symmetry and overall soundness. Absolutely free of legginess, profusely coated all over. A thick-set muscular, able-bodied dog with a most intelligent expression. The natural outline should not be artificially changed by scissoring or clipping.

How well we can picture the 'finished' product – in fact, a word picture of the mature Bobtail. It was felt necessary to draw attention to the fact that Bobtails are a 'natural' breed, and shape, etc. should not be suggested by barbering. This was a direct result of the over-exaggerated appearance of some exhibits in recent times, with stripped-out and scissored necks and shoulders, back-combed toplines and artificially shaped hindquarters.

Characteristics Of great stamina, exhibiting a gently rising topline and a pear-shaped body when viewed from above. The gait has a typical roll when ambling or walking. Bark has a distinctive toned quality.

In a working breed, one looks for the endurance that is required for a full day's work, over all terrain, in all weathers. The rising topline is something that one finds in a few pastoral breeds, perhaps the Rough Collie being the only other one to call for a rise. The body shape, when viewed from above, is quite distinctive with a definite narrowing from the breadth of the hindquarters towards the shoulder and front. The movement is also something quite special to the Bobtail, and the rolling gait can be compared to a big shaggy bear when ambling along. Much has been written and spoken about the bark. In the old days, it was described as 'pot-casse' – nobody could describe just what the term meant, and no general canine reference tome was helpful – so we describe it as having a peculiar distinctive note or tone. At any rate, the Bobtail's bark is certainly not like that of any other breed!

Temperament A biddable dog of even disposition. Bold, faithful and trustworthy, with no suggestion of nervousness or unprovoked aggression.

In all working dogs, it is essential that they should be of equable temper and willing to do as commanded. They must show a certain amount of calm plus courage, and be the faithful and trusty companion of their master, who may well be the herdsman or shepherd. A nervous or aggressive dog would not be able to face up to obstinate or panicky charges in the manner demanded of the owner's 'right hand'. An aggressive dog could not be trusted to care, as demanded, for the flock or herd, and so would be useless.

Head and Skull In proportion to the size of body. Skull capacious, rather square. Well arched above eyes, stop well defined. Muzzle strong, square and truncated, measuring approximately half of the total head length. Nose large and black. Nostrils wide.

In recent years we have come on such wide variations in heads, ranging from small and weak to a few which were patently gross-looking on a smaller neck and body. Therefore, the head must be part of a balanced, overall picture. The skull should be capacious enough to carry the brain of a worker, and if too narrow, we may find that the upper jaw formation will follow on by being narrow. It is my belief that this shortcoming has developed in the breed, for we are now finding too many exhibits whose rear teeth on the upper jaw are in direct opposition to those of the lower jaw, with the consequence that the mouth cannot close naturally. The next indication of

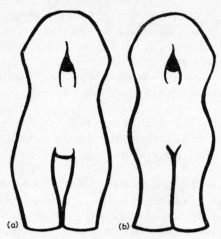

Figure 4   Faults of the forelegs
(a) out at elbow   (b) elbows 'tied in'

this serious fault then appears to be a tongue which is perpetually hanging out. A well-known geneticist has expressed the view that faults in dentition are some of the worst to deal with, for though they may remain hidden for a generation or two, he is convinced that they cannot be totally bred-out.

There must be strength in the Bobtail head, and this comes from the solidly built length, depth, and width which allows for the well formed arch over the eyes, the necessary width of the muzzle – and a good depth to it, which means there would be strong upper and lower jaws.

In the old Standard, a comparison was made to the Deerhound, which has a much weaker formation with a shallow face and no well-defined stop. Now that references to other breeds have been removed, it is essential that we know clearly the desired points, and how to assess them.

In more modern times, the Bobtail went through a stage where a massive skull and a little short muzzle seemed to be the fashion. That dentition faults followed is not surprising. To allow for a strong, balanced foreface there has to be a degree of length and when one refers to pictures of the original show dogs there can be no misunderstanding on this point. The Kennel Club is insistent that breeds should be reproduced without any exaggerations which can lead to faults, and there now seems to be a sensible description of an acceptable head. A large nose, with well-opened nostrils, is another essential for a dog that is to be fit and able to cover long distances quite fast. It is important that he should not be denied the ability to breathe easily.

Eyes Set well apart. Dark or wall-eyes. Two blue eyes acceptable, light eyes undesirable. Pigmentation on the eye rims preferred.

The breed needs sight over a wide area when looking after a large number of charges, and close-set eyes would prevent full and easy surveillance. There has been much argument over the term 'wall-eyes' so perhaps we should make sure there are no further misunderstandings. 'Wall-eye' means one eye that is blue and the other brown. There is no such thing as 'double wall-eyes'. The correct term is blue (or sometimes the word used is 'china'). Dark brown or wall-eye is preferable to two blue eyes, or light brown eyes. It is up to the judge to place a value on the eye qualities in relation to the rest of the dog, for we should assess the animal as a whole, and not 'knock' it merely because we are fault-finding and one particular point displeases us. Sometimes, breed specialist judges feel so strongly about a particular point that it is surely difficult for them to assess a dog's overall quality – more so than with an all-rounder who tends not to make such a fetish of particular points.

For years, reference to eyes was minimal, and I do feel that this part of the Standard is now much more helpful. Eyes can enhance, or spoil, the expression of a dog, especially young stock which has not yet grown a full head-covering of hair. At no time does the Standard give a fault, but merely emphasizes which points should be given preference, with light eyes not to be preferred. Though two blue eyes are acceptable, again they are not to be preferred. Unpigmented rims can be accepted, but again it is to be preferred that rims are pigmented. In detailing what is most preferable, the wording does allow for the not-so-perfect to be accepted.

Ears   Small, and carried flat to side of head.

To find a neat, small ear, carried correctly, is indeed a joy. So many are now far too large, and almost Spaniel-like. A large heavy ear, with its subsequent heavy coat, can lead to internal problems from poor ventilation.

Mouth   Teeth strong, large, and evenly placed. Scissor-bite – jaws strong with a perfect, regular and complete scissor bite, i.e. the upper teeth closely overlapping the lower teeth, and set square to the jaws. Pincer tolerated, but un-desirable.

This is a good description of the desirable. There are still some who ask for a pincer-bite, but against this bite is the fact that,

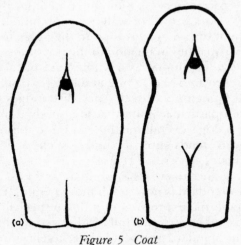

Figure 5   Coat
(a) excessive coat – shapeless outline
(b) correct amount of coat – workmanlike outline

when the edges of the teeth are opposed to each other, they will inevitably wear down. Also, it is not unknown for a level pincer-bite to end up by turning undershot. The value of a tight scissor-bite is that the upper teeth hold the lower teeth *firmly*, hence the lower jaw cannot subsequently slip forward, into the undershot position.

Neck   Fairly long, strong, arched gracefully.

The head of a dog which needs to survey a flock or a herd needs to be carried fairly high. With the weight of a good head upon it, we want reasonable neck length plus strength. A nicely arched neck invariably sets well into a good shoulder placement.

Forequarters   Forelegs perfectly straight, with plenty of bone, holding body well from ground. Elbows fitting close to brisket. Shoulders should be well laid back, being narrower at the point of withers than at the point of shoulder. Loaded shoulder undesirable. Dog standing lower at withers than loin.

Well-boned, strong, straight legs need no further clarification. Worth noting is that there must be length of leg, for with distance to travel, short legs would tire too easily. The requirements for the whole of the front, starting up on the withers with a well-angled joint at the point of the shoulder, then with straight, strong front legs into a springy pastern give the ideal forehand construction, as illustrated in Figure 1. The angulation can be likened to the suspension in a motor car. If there were no lay-back of shoulder, a short upper arm, no angle into elbow, and lack of pastern angle, then the dog would experience shock every time the foot hit the ground. The angulation gives the spring in the action, providing a built-in shock-absorber. Invariably, poorly laid shoulders will be linked to a short bullock-type neck, and a wider-than-desired coarse front. In maturity, such fronts will go wide, impairing correct, easy, tireless action. 'Loaded' shoulder means 'heavy'.

That the dog should be lower at the withers than loin, gives us the called-for rising topline.

Body   Rather short, and compact, with well-sprung ribs, and deep capacious brisket.

This description emphasizes the need for a square-looking body, viewed from the side. There is need for ample spring of rib, as the breed needs sufficient heart and lung room. A narrow and shallow brisket would restrict the expansion of the lungs, thus depriving the dog of its ability to sustain long, and strenuous, periods of exercise.

Hindquarters   Loin very sturdy, broad and gently arched, quarters well covered, round and muscular, the second thigh is long and well developed, the stifle well turned, and the hocks set low. From the rear, the hocks should be quite straight, with the feet turning neither in nor out.

In a strongly built dog, powerful hindquarters are of utmost importance for it is in this area that the muscle helps to push the dog along. I think that the wording describes the whole section very well. A low-set hock is very important, for it is from its strong joint that the impetus comes. A tall hock, perhaps lacking strength of joint, is often allied to a poorly angled stifle, giving only a weak hind action. One thing which I have found disturbing when judging over the past year or so is the increasing incidence of weak hock joints. To me, they are best likened to a double joint, for when pressure is exerted on the joint from behind, it will slop forward, going completely straight. Invariably, this weak hock joint is allied to lack of, or total absence of, muscle higher up in the leg. When the dog is moving, it is apparent that it is cosmetically 'carrying' the leg, rather than making full mechanical use of it. This weakened leg has nothing to induce it to muscle-up, with consequent poor hind action. When one hock is so affected, then the uneven hind movement is obvious, but should both hock joints be affected the movement, though untypical, is even, and the skilful handler will probably manage to move the exhibit so fast that the judge can effectively be fooled.

At this stage, I have little documentation, but it does appear to be a matter of concern. It has been suggested that there may be an element of heredity involved, but as yet there is insufficient pedigree evidence to back up such a claim.

That feet should point forward is common sense, for feet turning out will lessen the strength of the thrust from the hindquarters.

Feet   Small, round and tight, toes well arched, pads thick and hard. Dew claws should be removed.

Feet are very important in a breed that will depend on them through so much of its life. Small feet which are well rounded and not spread out will be surer for working and for agility in insecure places. Well arched toes will ensure a good grip, whilst the well-padded under-part will make for more comfortable, effortless walking and running. To ensure that feet do not start to spread, I cut back quite hard the toenails on puppies from a very early age – even as young as seven to ten days old. Flat, spread feet can develop through lack of exercise on suitable surfaces. Soft mud, sand, or gravel will not help with tightening up of feet. Poor, thin pads will not stand up to long exercise over varying terrain, and are more subject to splitting and soreness.

Gait/Movement   When walking, exhibits a bear-like roll from the rear. When trotting, shows effortless extension and strong driving rear action, with legs moving straight along line of travel. Very elastic at the gallop. At slow speeds, some dogs may tend to pace. When moving, the head carriage may adopt a naturally lower position.

The movement of the Bobtail is quite distinctive and, as pointed out earlier under 'Characteristics', easily compared to a bear with its ambling, rolling action. It has been accepted that with the rising topline and strong hindquarters, the dog's action is rather special, and can't be compared to that of most other pastoral breeds, which have a level topline.

The trotting movement is one that covers the ground easily, with great fluidity. As the Bobtail needs to cover long distances, good conformation is paramount, starting off with good fore-quarters, and well angulated and formed hindquarters. The good angles allow for the extension of the joints, thus allowing the dog to cover ample distance with little effort. The need for the legs to move directly along the line of travel means that the dog will not waste energy in excess action of its limbs. Elasticity is also important, for should the action be taut and jerky, it would be tiring. Some judges will penalize very heavily the dog that paces. I cannot agree with this, though I do also require to see a dog 'break' the pace and move in the conventional manner. (Pacing is when an animal moves the legs on each side, in a parallel manner.) A pacing dog will exhibit an accen-tuated roll, which should not be confused with the typical 'Bobtail roll'. Pacing is an energy-conserving gait, often used by horses when they have a long hard journey ahead, therefore an intelligent working dog should not be discarded for moving thus.

Many of the pastoral breeds tend to drop the head, perhaps to the level of the back, when moving. After all, they need to see the surfaces ahead, so it would be unnatural for them to hold their heads up.

Tail   Customarily completely docked.

This is perhaps the most controversial part of many breed standards at the time of writing. The tail of the OES has traditionally been 'bobbed', and the thought of an OES with a long bushy tail is abhorrent to many. However, at present there are strong moves in the Council of Europe to prohibit the removal of tails. A strong lobby is operating in the UK, and the Kennel Club has been advised, in no uncertain terms, as to the strong wish to retain the right to dock. On the other side of the argument, there are those who wish to leave tails in their natural state, and they are strongly supported by an increasing number of members of the veterinary profession. Should the legislation be forced through, there will be a further problem – that of the tail set and carriage. In a breed that does not call for a sloping croup, one envisages a high-set tail. In the pastoral breeds, when judging, we look for a low tail carriage, not rising above the level of the back. With the envisaged OES tail-set, I cannot imagine a low tail carriage. The attraction of many to the OES has been due to its chunky tail-less appearance, and I feel that there may not be such demand if we are to forgo the removal of that long and very bushy appendage.

Coat Profuse, of good hard texture, not straight, but shaggy and free from curl. Undercoat of waterproof pile. Head and skull well covered with hair, ears moderately coated, neck well coated, forelegs well coated all round, hindquarters more heavily coated than rest of body. Quality, texture, and profusion to be considered above mere length.

Coat is of great importance, for a dog expected to be out in all weathers must have a wind-and-waterproof jacket, well insulated. A straight, lank coat would be incorrect, as would one that is curly. Here we are seeking a happy medium in that it should have a 'break' to the texture. This is hard to define, but I would describe it as having 'movement'. The fully coated Bobtail, well groomed, is a joy to behold, but for those who do not wish to exhibit, it is perhaps helpful to keep the coat regularly combed-through, in order to reduce the amount of undercoat. Dogs kept outdoors will need all the undercoat they can grow for winter warmth, but for those who live indoors, there is no need to retain so much. The detail in the coat clause gives the varying amounts of coat that is desirable on specific parts of the dog, and it is this which gives the mature, finished OES its distinctive shape and appearance. It is good to see that the emphasis is now on the quality and texture of the coat. We saw in the early 1960s many Bobtails with sufficient coats of correct weatherproof quality, which were not at all overdone. Then appearances started to alter, with some show dogs being exhibited in overly-long coats, sometimes obviously clipped and shaped, to deceive on appearance – and possibly to camouflage faults! Now some twenty-five years later, commonsense seems to be prevailing, with greater consideration being given to *quality* of coat rather than *quantity*.

> *Colour*   Any shade of grey, grizzle or blue. Body and hind-quarters of solid colour, with or without white socks. White patches in the solid area to be discouraged. Head, neck, forequarters and under belly to be white, with or without markings. Any shade of brown undesirable.

The question of coat colour never fails to be a topic of conversation, which sometimes becomes quite heated! The present-day popular conception of the most attractive coat colour seems to be blue, but as long as the quality is good, there is no need to penalise a dog for being either darker or lighter than this. The silver dog is not quite so attractive, as it does not contrast so well against the white parts. It is good that the brown coat is stated to be undesirable, and some non-breed judges would do well to carefully study the Breed Standard! At certain times, some brown may appear in the coat, but this is normally the dead hair which is best removed without delay in order to enable the new coat to grow in. In old age also, the coat sometimes tends to brown towards the tips and at the hocks.

One rarely sees a breeder showing an animal which has 'flashed' markings, i.e. with white patches on the blue whole colour of the body coat, yet these pups are often sold as show specimens at comparatively high prices. One will rarely find a judge, particularly a breed specialist, who will highly place any dog with very obvious large white patches, often called mismarks. It seems very cruel to cut short the life of any puppy so marked, but it is not unknown for a breeder to decide that such an animal should be put down. An alternative, in Britain, should the breeders decide they do not want it to be shown, or bred from, is to sell at a pet price, with endorsed papers. To prevent this arrangement from being abused, it is possible to ask the Kennel Club to endorse the dog's registration certificate (and their records) to the effect that the animal is not for exhibition, neither will its progeny be eligible for registration.

Thus, if anyone tried to register the progeny from a badly marked parent they would find that they are prevented from registering it at the Kennel Club; and in these more enlightened days, most people like to be certain that an animal for which they are going to pay quite a high price is 'Kennel Club Registered' before agreeing to purchase. Feeling on the subject of the so-called mis-mark (correctly referred to as 'flashed') is beginning to run fairly high in Britain and I hear also in parts of Europe and the Antipodes. I understand that in America it is not uncommon to see flashed stock being placed favourably in competition.

Size 24″ and upwards for dogs, 22″ and upwards for bitches. Type and symmetry of greatest importance, and on no account to be sacrificed to size alone.

For some time, we seemed to experience great diversity in size but over the last few years it seems to have levelled off. In past years we have seen some very large, impressive-looking dogs, and the reverse, but now the line-ups in the more senior breed classes carry an obvious improvement overall. Way back in 1905, Aubrey Hopwood stated that his ideal would be 24½ inches in height (to the shoulder). Champion Reculver Little Rascal was 24 inches at the shoulder, and was at times classed as 'small'. Devotees will have made up their own minds as to whether they prefer the smaller, compact animal or the larger and rangier type. Clients from abroad should make certain that the type of stock they are seeking will be that bred by their supplier. But it is the responsibility of the breeder to show his honesty and integrity by ensuring that the export is as near to the order as humanly possible. The overseas buyer will usually want an undertaking that the stock is free of hip dysplasia and probably also of eye troubles. In the case of a puppy, the breeder can give an assurance only that its parents and perhaps a few generations before them were free of hip dysplasia. However, with an adult (over thirteen months old) it is possible to get a more positive opinion. Unfortunately, eye troubles are becoming more common and apparently clear stock may well be carrying the genes, which may be reproduced in later breedings. Consequently, no guarantee can honestly be given.* If photographs are not available a full description will often help the purchaser to decide, taking into account the background breeding, if the breeder has what he wants. It is quite wrong to adopt the attitude that as the customer is far away, a breeder can send anything and 'get away with it'. Modern communications being so efficient, it is possible that at some time in the future breeder and buyer may come face to face! Each year, the crowds around the rings at the larger Championship shows increase, with a goodly sprinkling of visitors from overseas. They are as well informed as anyone, and have to work hard for and save their money as we do, so *do not* ever think that they can be 'taken for a ride'. Shipping a puppy to its destination, with all the necessary documentation, can often cost several times the purchase price, so it must be worthy of exporting.

Overseas customers are normally very patient, and if you as a breeder explain to them when you receive their enquiry that you are currently unable to help, but anticipate being able to do so within the next few months, they will usually be willing to wait. If you panic and try to get hold of whatever is available at the time of an enquiry, which is not exactly what is wanted, the probable result is a disillusioned purchaser who will not come to you again for fear of similar treatment.

Faults Any departure from the points should be considered a fault, and the seriousness with which the fault

---

*It is now possible to have eyes tested, and a certificate issued (in a similar manner to the Hip Dysplasia Scheme), under the joint Kennel Club/British Veterinary Association schemes for Hereditary Cataract and Progressive Retinal Atrophy.

should be regarded should be in exact proportion to its degree.

Here, the onus is now placed on the judge to assess the degree of fault, making an overall judgment of the dog. In the past, points were awarded for various virtues, but it hardly seemed right to judge dogs by adding up a points score.

Note Male animals should have two apparently normal testicles fully descended into the scrotum.

The last two clauses of the Breed Standard are compulsory for all breeds.

3

Finding and Choosing a Puppy

BEFORE rushing off post-haste to buy the first puppy you hear about, please stop and think carefully. There are various reasons for wanting a Bobtail, but once it is yours it will become a part of your family for many years, so a little forethought will ensure that the first steps are in the right direction. Having made up your mind that this is *the* breed for you, I suggest you try to make contact with one or two local breeders. If this is difficult, you can write to the Kennel Club, or to the Secretary of the Breed Club most likely to cover your area. Your local veterinary surgeon may also know of any breeders in the locality.

Once you establish contact with a breeder, do admit that you are seeking advice and help, and ask him to spare you some time so that you can see not only grown animals, but possibly others at intermediate stages. This will be the time for you to ask the thousand and one questions on your mind. If, when you meet up with the Bobtail breeder-enthusiast, you feel that after all, the breed is more than you can cope with, *please* admit that this is so – you will be respected for your honesty. This is a rare occurrence, but better that such a decision is made beforehand rather than afterwards.

When you visit a breeder (or enthusiastic owner), ask him to show you what is entailed in grooming and caring for the fully-coated dog; a puppy with smooth, short hair gives no indication of the profuse jacket that will rapidly grow in the months to come. Find out all you can about diet, and how much feeding costs from puppyhood through to maturity. Check on exercise too: if only a small garden is available, this need not be a deterrent so long as adequate space is accessible when the puppy needs more exercise. Consider carefully whether your domestic commitments will allow you to give a Bobtail the attention that it demands. If father is often away from home, leaving mother to cope with young children plus a growing, boisterous puppy, then a year or two's delay may be best from all viewpoints. You must be prepared to give a certain amount of time to your puppy each and every day. Growing puppies need regular attention and love, like children; they are *not* toys to be smothered with affection one day, and ignored the next. (I usually tell visitors that if they have successfully raised happy, healthy children, then they should do well with an Old English Sheepdog – they are so alike in many respects!)

Another piece of well-founded advice is that it is better to have a puppy after the arrival of the first baby, rather than before. The period between the wife's stopping work and the arrival of a first-born may seem ideal for the purchase of a puppy, and in some ways it is, for the puppy can have lots of love and attention; however, there comes a time of sudden change for the pup when the doting owner goes to hospital, or is confined to bed at home for the birth. His feeling of security can be impaired, as she will not be with him and looking after him for maybe two weeks, and when she is about again she will have another interest. Little puppy, having previously had undivided attention, will not understand the new routine, and may try to draw attention to the fact that he is still around by frequent puddles, or chewing forbidden things. In my opinion, it is during the first few months after the birth of the baby, when it only needs feeding and changing and sleeps for much of the time, that is ideal for the arrival of a new puppy. It will come into a house where there is already a baby, and so will accept the whole set-up. The arrival of subsequent children does not appear to affect the family dog, as by then he is more mature. I speak from experience in this matter, for our daughter was some three months old when we purchased our first Old English Sheepdog, who adored her until the day he died and was a constant guard over her pram when in the garden. Never far from her as she grew up, they were great pals until the end. I am not suggesting that this is the *only* way to work in the acquisition of a puppy; there are, of course, exceptions which have also worked out perfectly well.

I assumed earlier that you would be able to contact a local breeder for help, advice and possible purchase of your Bobtail, but if there is no one available locally there are other courses of action.

Try to find out when there will be a Dog Show within reach of your home, at which there will be classes for Old English Sheepdogs. All-breed Championship Shows now have such classes, and this can involve the attendance of between 100 and 150 owner-exhibitors. Some of the larger local Canine Societies also have these at their shows, but not on the scale of the Championship events. The Old English Sheepdog Breed Clubs also put on shows each year, confined to the breed.

Details of future events can be obtained from the nearest Breed Club Secretary, or you may find it useful to get one of the dog specialist journals, *Our Dogs* or *Dog World*. These weekly papers carry advertisements for forthcoming shows, and the writers of 'Breed Notes' (a regular feature) often refer to forthcoming events in their own particular breed.

When you have decided which show to visit, try to get there in time to sit by the ringside, and watch the judging. This will enable you to see Bobtails in all stages of growth and development, as puppies may be shown from six months of age and there is no upper age limit. You will be surprised at the varied colours – some of the very young puppies will still be carrying much of their black baby coat, others will appear 'patchy' where in one part the adult blue coat is just growing through the receding puppy black, and in another the mature coat is of rich blue-grey – beautiful, even coloured and profuse. On arrival, please resist the temptation (unless invited!) to rush up and start talking to an exhibitor who is obviously trying to prepare his dog for the show ring. Bent double, attempting to clean probably grubby feet, and the white parts, prior to grooming, the average owner will not be anxious to engage in lengthy conversation. Better to stand quietly by, and watch, and if not in too much of a hurry they may ask if you are interested in the breed, and be prepared to tell you a little about what they are doing, but at this stage on a show day let them take the initiative. The time to seek help and advice is when all the judging of the immaculate exhibits is completed. The rush is over, and they should be able to give you the undivided attention which – I am happy to say – is typical of most enthusiasts.

On entering the show, buy a catalogue in which all the exhibitors and their dogs will be listed, together with addresses, so you should then have no trouble in finding one or two fairly near your home. Each exhibit is given a number in the catalogue, which is also worn by the handler when in the ring and displayed above the dog's bench, so identification is easy at any stage of the show.

You may feel that you want to go to several shows before finally deciding where to get your puppy. If you are likely to become ambitious, and want your puppy to be of possible show quality, not merely a house-dog, then certain breeders' dogs will appeal to you more than others. Bobtail folk are a friendly crowd, and you will soon be getting the information you need.

We will now assume that you have definitely decided to purchase a puppy, but whatever happens, *don't* buy from dealers. Those who offer a multiplicity of breeds cannot be called Bobtail specialists, since for them dogs are merely a business where litters are often bought in wholesale, at anything from five to six weeks of age, for subsequent re-sale. Using the methods I have suggested, you should be able to contact a bona-fide breeder. The true Bobtail breeder will only use sound stock. Nowadays, when hereditary defects can be found in almost every breed, conscientious breeders will have their stock carefully checked to ensure that it does not show any of these. Bobtails have not escaped a share of such troubles and eye problems, hip dysplasia, occasional deafness, defects in dentition and poor back-ends are not unknown. A good breeder will have had the bitch X-rayed before arranging for the breeding of a litter to ensure that the hips are quite sound and properly formed; he will then mate the bitch to a carefully selected stud dog, who has also been X-rayed and certified clear of H.D. Eyes will also have been checked by a *qualified* ophthalmologist.

Do not expect breeders to invite an invasion of visitors to peer at newly born puppies. I never allow anyone apart from the family to see them until they are at least five weeks old, and even then it is only to look – *not* to pick up and handle. The breeder who had done everything possible to guarantee cleanliness and hygiene will not wish to risk possible infection being brought in to the still vulnerable puppies. A proud and helpful breeder will let you pay more than one visit, so that you can observe the litter and their tremendous rate of growth. From these visits, it is to be hoped that you will have seen the nice clean way in which the pups are being reared, the happy atmosphere in the kennels, and the general air of well-being about the whole set-up.

If your breeder is one of experience and long standing, it will pay to rely on his/her advice when selecting your puppy. Be quite honest when you place your order, and state if you only want a house-dog that will never be taken near the show ring, in which case you obviously wish to pay a pet price. If you are seeking a puppy that you can probably take to a few local shows, as a means of enjoyment, then do say so. No breeder likes to see a pup which for various reasons has been graded as of pet quality, being rushed into the show ring.

Equally, if you want to get going with a show-quality dog, then please make this equally clear. The careful breeder grades each litter, and charges accordingly. Remember that they have all been carefully reared, but there is bound to be room for improvement on one or two points in some cases. For instance, a head may be narrower than strictly desirable in a show dog, or perhaps the back is a fraction longer than ideal. Mouth is an important point to check, and a jaw that shows a definite fault by eight weeks of age will rarely correct itself. These things influence the grading of 'show' and 'pet' quality.

Price is always a matter for debate, but the popular current pet price seems to be in the region of £125 upwards, with dogs of show potential going for approximately £175 and upwards. These should not be taken as concrete figures, because everyone has different ideas on the value of their dogs, but are intended as a rough guide to intending purchasers.

The subject of 'flashed' (or in America referred to as 'splashed') Bobtails will be discussed at greater length later in the book, but a puppy carrying a very noticeable patch, or stripes, of white on the blue body parts, is described as 'flashed', and some breeders will sell these as pets only, at very reasonable prices to good homes. The breeder who does not care for flashes will sometimes go to the trouble of asking the Kennel Club to endorse the registration card to the effect that the animal is not to be exhibited. This is not unreasonable, especially if the price has been reduced accordingly.

Naturally, the most difficult puppy to pick out is the show dog. If you have placed yourself in the hands of an experienced breeder, then trust him, for it is in his interests that the reputation of his breed-line should be upheld by a good specimen in the show ring. If your breeder is a novice, then perhaps the owner of the stud dog will be able to help him with the grading and selection of the best stock. Should this not prove possible, however, I offer you a few salient points to check when trying to pick out the best on your own. All the puppies should be bright and happy, with clear eyes and no sign of runny noses or mucus round the eyes. The ears should be sweet, with no discharge. Avoid any puppy that is 'droopy' compared with the others; it may be that it will never be bold enough to become a confident show dog. Carefully check that the head is nice and broad, and the ears not too large at this stage; they should be small, and held close to the head.

The muzzle should be truncated and rather square, at this age, with no signs of being 'foxy'. The mouth and teeth should also be examined – not an easy job, but carefully and firmly done to see the set of the teeth. The Breed Standard calls for a 'scissor bite', which means that the top teeth fit tightly but just overlap the bottom row. A puppy with an undershot mouth, where the bottom teeth project beyond the top, is not a good choice as a show prospect. Remember that a mouth which

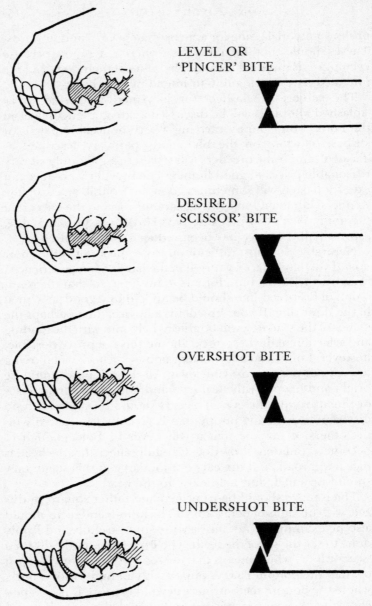

LEVEL OR
'PINCER' BITE

DESIRED
'SCISSOR' BITE

OVERSHOT BITE

UNDERSHOT BITE

Figure 6   The bite

shows this fault at around eight weeks is unlikely to correct into a perfect bite.

In general appearance, the head of a good puppy can be compared to that of a Clumber Spaniel, ears excepted. They have a similar expression. Check that the head is set atop a fair length of neck growing into a shortish, compact body, with a back that does not appear elongated. Ideally, the overall picture of the body is squarish and sturdy, with nothing to suggest a Whippet-type shape. Good bone is absolutely essential, and is achieved by sensible pre-natal feeding and suitable additives given to the in-whelp bitch, plus adequate supplies while she was feeding the litter. The frontal appearance should be straight, with no bow-leggedness, and the hind legs should show some angulation, with no sign of cow-hocks.

The coat should be clean, dense and glossy. A dull coat is

Figure 7   The head

(a) head broad; eyes 1½ times their width apart; arch of cheek bone fairly straight under eye, but curves away towards back; nose large and capacious

(b) marked stop; ears set on side of skull (continue an imaginary line from lower eye-lid to give correct placing); end of muzzle gives the impression of being 'cut off' abruptly

Figure 8   Square proportion – in profile

not a good sign, and coupled with a pot-belly should make one suspect the presence of worms. The breeder should have wormed the bitch and her litter when the pups were six weeks old, and again at seven and a half weeks of age. (More information on the treatment of worms etc. can be found in the chapter on ailments.)

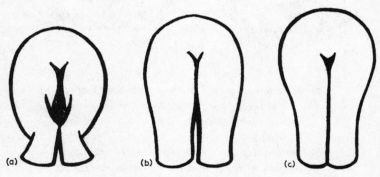

Figure 9   Hindlegs
(a) cow hocks   (b) correct   (c) close behind

Check that the puppy does not have an umbilical hernia. This is not serious, usually being caused when the bitch insists on tugging at the umbilical cord during birth instead of allowing the owner to cut it cleanly. The hernia appears like a tiny pea of soft flesh in the middle of the tummy. If this happens to any of my puppies, my vet attends to them before they go to new homes; it is only a minute incision, and stitching-up, that is required. Some breeders disregard an umbilical hernia, but, if this is pointed out, may possibly make an allowance on the price, so that you can have this attended to later on if you choose. If not attended to, such a hernia will rarely grow any larger, but should be carefully observed for a time in order to ensure that it is not going to cause any future trouble; great care *must* also be taken when grooming in these circumstances, to ensure that the hernia is not 'caught' by the teeth of a comb.

Pigmentation is more important in the prospective show dog than in the family pet. Puppies are born with pink noses, lips and eye-rims, the first sign of the black pigmentation appearing after about the first week in the form of faint bluish coloured spots on the nose. Some puppies seem to get their black noses much faster than others. When ready to leave at eight weeks, they are sometimes carrying what is referred to as a 'butterfly' nose, which has a distinctly mottled appearance; these noses usually fill in fairly quickly, but a puppy who still has a really pink nose at this stage may be very much slower. In Bobtails with all-white heads, the pigmentation is frequently very slow to appear around the eye-rims, and in some cases may never completely meet all round. The subject of pigmentation is regarded more seriously in Europe than in Britain, and great pains are taken to check this as carefully as dentition.

Markings depend very much on particular breed-lines, for some seem to carry heavier amounts of blue coat than others. The popular marking is for the greater part of the head to be white, with a shawl and front (right down to the feet) also white, plus white feet or socks to the rear. There is no need to be so particular about the markings of the family pet, but in the show dog certain forms of marking can give a misleading impression of the actual body shape. Lack of a white shawl on the neck and back, towards the shoulders, suggests an illusion of a long back and lack of neck, whereas this may not be so at all. A study of the exhibits in the show ring will illustrate the most attractive markings. A good judge of the breed will not be unduly influenced by markings, being more concerned with what is beneath them. As long as the coat's colour, texture and length are pleasing, a dog which is not so attractively marked will most probably be placed favourably if it satisfies them in all other respects. The not-so-expert judge will possibly be unable to resist the better-marked dogs when it comes to final placings, something we are finding on the increase!

A superbly groomed and attractively marked Old English Sheepdog, showing his paces in grand style, cannot fail to catch the eye of the judge of the Working Group, and maybe that of the Best in Show judge, at the Championship Shows. There have been many Bobtails who have won Groups, and quite a few who can claim to have been placed Best in Show, Reserve Best in Show or Best Opposite Sex in Show at leading events in the show year. It is no longer a rare occurrence for one of the breed to take the top award at Open Shows as well as the smaller ones.

Some breeders ask their vet to check over the entire litter before they will let the pups go, and each purchaser may then receive a Certificate of Health. Not everyone does this, therefore if you want the puppy vetted before parting with your hard-earned cash, you must reasonably expect to pay for this yourself.

In the next chapter, we go on to deal with the preparations necessary for taking your puppy home and settling him in, also the question of his diet, training and so on.

4

The New Puppy

BEFORE setting out to collect your puppy, I would advise that you take with you a couple of good absorbent towels; these can be put on your lap underneath him for the trip home, just in case of an accident! When you arrive at the kennels, you will have some details to attend to before you actually collect the new member of your family. Most breeders register their litters with the Kennel Club before the puppies are old enough to go to their new homes, and you will receive the official Registration Certificate which incorporates a section for transfer of ownership, which the breeder will have signed. (You should complete your part of the form, and forward it to the Kennel Club with the appropriate fee, to keep the records straight.) The breeder should also supply the puppy's pedigree, which is usually over five generations, and may contain some well-known Champions of the past and present. A conscientious breeder will ensure that you do not leave without a comprehensive diet sheet, *and* that you fully understand it. I normally give new owners some of the food with which I have been feeding the puppy, so that it does not experience too great a change. It can be a great help to have enough meat for a couple of days, plus sufficient puppy meal to last about a week until you can locate the supply of the right type. It is sensible too to make sure that you have a supply of the calcium, vitamins, etc., that your puppy has been having.

When paying for your new acquisition, it is reasonable to expect a receipt, and if any sort of breeding arrangement is made at the time of sale this should all be written out and signed by both parties concerned. For example, it may be agreed that the breeder should have a say in the stud to be used for her first litter (in the case of a bitch), and possibly the choice of a puppy from that mating, either at a nominal charge or in some cases with no charge at all. Where a male is concerned, the breeder may sometimes have one or two free studs from him, or may even have some control over the entire stud life of the dog if it is of very special breeding. This is not general practice, but may happen sometimes when a puppy is sold at a reduced price for this specific purpose. Some breeders are unable to keep all the stock that they would wish, and this is one way in which they can maintain an interest in the next generation of their breeding.

Once all the paper work is completed, you are ready to set off home with the puppy. If the journey is a long one, see that he has previously had a light meal, but not too near to the time of the trip. If you manage to get him to do a puddle before starting off, there is every hope that you will reach home with a dry lap! Should you be fortunate enough to own a puppy box, or have a friend who will lend you one, it will be an easier drive home for everyone. Sometimes it is necessary for a puppy to be sent by rail, but in these days it is a very hazardous undertaking. One hears of puppies being off-loaded at the wrong destination, etc., and I would earnestly advise that you do all in your power to collect your pup personally. I have often heard of young stock being sent by air quite successfully within the United Kingdom, and here they appear to receive every consideration.

However you transport your pup, do try to make it a quiet and peaceful homecoming. It will all be rather bewildering, coming to a strange place, having endured the journey after leaving familiar mother and the rest of the brothers and sisters, so please make certain that there is not a large 'welcome committee' of neighbours and relatives, however kindly meant. Allow the pup to have a quiet nose around to familiarize himself with the new surroundings before offering him something light as a first meal. I normally advise warmed milk in which glucose has been dissolved (1 dessertspoon to half a pint of milk), this being gently poured over some cereal. This is sufficient for the first couple of hours, when you can start to feed him according to the diet sheet. For the first day or two, I feed smallish meals, slightly more often than stated, since food means security and that is just what the youngster needs. By then, the puppy should have settled down to eating quite normally.

Give careful consideration to sleeping arrangements. If the warm weather has meant that the litter have been hardened off and accustomed to sleeping outdoors in an airy kennel, to be brought indoors into stuffy conditions can make a restless puppy, so before you leave the breeder do ascertain just where your puppy has been kept at night and try to create a similar atmosphere for a while until the settling-in period is over.

If the weather is cold, make sure that wherever the puppy sleeps it is quite dry and free from draughts. I do not think dog beds are worth considering with a Bobtail in view of their high cost, so I would advise starting with a large cardboard box, cutting a 'U' shape out of one side so that the pup can hop in and out without difficulty. Put in an old towel or piece of blanket on which he can snuggle down to sleep. If you first pick him up and put him into the box a few times, he will soon understand that this is where he is meant to rest. Wooden boxes can be chewed, with resultant sickness if splinters are swallowed, and old-fashioned wicker baskets can also be the cause of late-night calls to the vet. When I was younger we had a Wire-haired Fox Terrier who almost died through having an intestine pierced by a strand of wicker. I would never advocate the use of wood wool as bedding for puppies; if a puddle is made in the bed it can easily be seen on a piece of towelling or blanket, but would just disappear through anything else, so for the sake of hygiene do choose your bedstuffs carefully.

The questions of where to keep your puppy must also be carefully considered. In the first few weeks you will experience some inconvenience by having to mop up puddles at odd times, so to make things easier I would advise keeping him where the floor can be washed without too much trouble. Once the pup is clean and trustworthy, you can let him venture on to precious carpets. Most people find it easiest to keep their puppy in the kitchen, where he can easily be put out of the back door at frequent intervals. Incidentally, if you do get a puddle on the carpet, the best way to neutralize the urine and prevent staining is to cover the area with a few squirts from a siphon of soda water. There will not be an enormous lake, so a siphon will last quite some time. Then gently mop up the excess moisture with kitchen paper or tissues, without rubbing; this should ensure that the patch dries out without any misplacement of the pile or discoloration.

From the time that the puppy comes home, give him his own feeding dishes, and always use these for him alone. I find that the old-fashioned glazed pottery ones are best; being heavy, the puppy cannot drag them around the floor and possibly flood it with his drinking water in the process. Modern plastic dishes are very light but so easily picked up to play with, and can also be chewed too easily for my liking. Similar arguments apply to the lightweight alloy or aluminium dishes, but here the danger in chewing them is that the jagged metal can so easily damage gums, tongue, etc. Two bowls are sufficient: one for water, of which there should always be a plentiful, clean supply; the other for meals, which should be removed as soon as the food is finished, or taken away if the food is not all eaten within about twenty minutes.

By the time a puppy leaves the kennels it is usually accustomed to three or four meals per day, in the proportion of two meat and two milk or else two meat and one milk. The conscientious breeder will ensure (as mentioned earlier) that you take with you a comprehensive diet and care sheet, with instructions to contact him if there is anything else you need to know or cannot understand. Our eight-week-old puppies have four meals a day, starting with breakfast; for this I mix one raw egg and a dessertspoon of powdered glucose into half a pint of milk which has been slightly warmed. This is then poured over the cereal (rice crispies, Weetabix or similar type). Some breeders use porridge exclusively, but there is little merit in puppies that are overweight and bloated in appearance. In fact, excessive weight is a handicap to the youngster's heart and soft growing bones.

Lunch is normally given after the family have had their mid-

(*C. M. Cooke*)

Ch Pastelblue Carol Ann

(*C. M. Cooke*)

Ch Reculver Sugar Bush

Pastelblue Precious
Maid
(*Thomas Fall*)

(*C. M. Cooke*)

Ch Beckington Lady of Welbyhouse

(C. M. Cooke)

Ch Prospect Shaggy Boy

(Thomas Fall)

Ch Rollingsea Ringleader and Ch Wrightway's Glorious Day

(*Diane Pearce*)

Ch Keyingham Double Daisy. Supreme Best in Show at Bournemouth Championship Show 1979 and top winning Old English Sheepdog for that year

Ch Fernville Special Style of Trushayp. Supreme Best in Show at Windsor and L.K.A. Championship Shows in 1975

day meal, and takes the form of raw or lightly cooked fresh meat into which is mixed some good quality puppy meal such as Wheatmeal. Tea is little more than a drink of milk, into which we stir a little Farex or other baby food. Supper is fed mid-evening, and is a repeat of the midday meat feed into which I mix the steamed bone flour that is given for bone growth, plus cod liver oil or halibut liver oil in either liquid or capsule form. When cooking meat, I only put a small amount of water into the bottom of the saucepan, and then heat the meat through gently so that it changes colour from bright red to a brownish tone. This is a personal preference, and some breeders only feed raw meat, but both methods seem to work quite well, so be advised by your breeder on this point.

Whatever happens, do not feed wet and sloppy meat; it should be just moist, and when the wheatmeal is mixed in the texture will be fairly firm. I never feed dry puppy meal, as the hungry pup can so easily end up with sore intestines if there happens to be a sharp edge to any of the wheatmeal pieces. The quantity of bone flour depends on the age of the puppy. At eight weeks we generally feed one dessertspoon per day, increasing to a tablespoon at six months, three dessertspoons at nine months, and two tablespoons from a year until the dog has obviously completed its growth at fifteen months or thereabouts. This is always fed in conjunction with the fish liver oil. Use one capsule daily until six months of age, then two daily until growth is completed. The adults are given the fish liver oil each winter, too. A vitamin/mineral supplement is also advised.

When our puppies are twelve weeks of age, they are usually ready to go on to three meals a day, i.e. the milk feed at breakfast, meat at midday, and meat again at night. From around 6 oz of meat per day at eight weeks of age, the amount needs to be increased in stages, until at six months they are usually ready to take about 1 lb daily, split between the two meals. At about nine months of age, we find it necessary to increase these quantities up to 1¼ lb, or possibly in the case of a male even to 1½lb. This diet should be watched carefully, as some animals need more than others, and as I have said previously, there is no merit in an overweight dog. We find that by the time they are eight months old, two meals per day is ample, i.e. giving a milk/cereal breakfast, and the rest mid-evening. This does not necessarily apply to all dogs, as some will be happy on the three meals until they are probably nine months. There are no hard and fast rules – common sense here is the best guide. Cheese is a useful and much-appreciated addition to the diet, as is fish. I have never used fish as a substitute for meat, but know of some dogs who love the change. Cheese can be easily added to meals, and on the odd occasion when we have been a bit short of meat, extra eggs and cheese have been happily accepted.

The addition of some proprietary product as an aid to coat growth is popular, and everyone has his own favourite. Seaweed powder is acclaimed by many as the best, whilst others use veterinary yeast, plenty of raw eggs, or other powders or tablets. Here again, I would advise you to consult your breeder. The suitability of bones is often raised. A piece of middle marrow bone is ideal, but here again some prefer that they should be raw while others bake them in the oven or gently stew them. Avoid small bones or those from poultry.

Worming is normally carried out by the breeder before the puppy leaves him, and I then advise that when the veterinary surgeon has given the second of the distemper immunization shots he should be asked for the correct worming tablets. The two best-known are called 'Citrazine' and 'Banacide', these being the names given to similar products by different drug houses. The dose is one tablet per 10 lb of body weight, correct to the nearest 5 lb *above* the body weight. So first weigh your puppy! This is not too difficult if you pick up the pup and weigh him with you, then weigh yourself separately and deduct from the combined weights to give an accurate figure. The dosing should be repeated after 12–14 days to ensure a complete clearance. Whilst the youngster is still growing, I repeat this operation every two months. In the old days, worming was an unpleasant business, with the poor creatures being starved off for a period before the actual dosing could take place, but in these more enlightened times the vermifuge can be safely given (crushed up into powder) in the meal.

When worming has been carried out, it is essential that the dog's motions are checked for the next few days, as the newer type of treatment causes the worms to be stunned, and after a time any expelled worms can sometimes been seen to be moving slightly. Always clear up any droppings immediately, as a curious animal may be inclined to sniff around, thus being in a position to start up the cycle all over again. The life cycle of the worm is such that if the second dosing is not carried out, any eggs left behind by the expelled worms will hatch, and can thus set up the infestation very quickly. Worms can be the cause of so many problems that this regular dosing is a *must* if you wish to ensure the continued good health of your puppy. Dull, staring coats, lack of appetite, ravenous appetite, pot-belly, sickness – any of these symptoms should immediately make one think of worms, so regular attention to this point will relieve the owner of some of these worries.

We have, up to now, assumed that the newly acquired addition to the family will be living indoors. Sometimes there are reasons why this is not possible, and so outdoor accommodation must be decided upon. A fairly roomy kennel, or small shed, with the base raised off the ground, is quite suitable. If it can be lined, this makes for better insulation in both summer and winter. We find that a stable door type of closure is ideal; with both doors open we can easily go in and out, and this is also good in hot weather; in the wet and wintry months, the top half can be closed, just leaving the bottom part open for the dog's access and egress. In my kennels the upper door accounts for about two-thirds of the length, the lower one being quite small but tall enough for a dog to enter without having to crawl on its belly. If you are able to design and make your own kennels, then a roof which slopes to the back is ideal as any moisture then drains away from the front.

Everyone has their own opinions about the most suitable surface for a run, which is best enclosed by chain-link fencing. From our own local merchants we have been able to obtain some very good, reasonably priced, porous concrete slabs about 1 foot square. They are easy to clean, as any excreta can be shovelled up quickly and easily, and they can be hosed and scrubbed down with no trouble, the porosity ensuring that the moisture soon drains through and dries out. Within twenty minutes of a really sharp rain shower, they are quite dry, and never strike as cold as concrete either. Our first pen was on grass, which soon became a muddy paddy-field in the hardest-used places, so we put a line of these slabs along the edge where the 'mad little mob' used to chase around, plus a good area just outside the door of the shed and up to the gateway. We soon found that a large litter could finish off grass almost overnight, so we reduced the size of the pen in order that it could be covered all over with the slabs. The surface helps to toughen up puppies' feet, and we rarely find that nails need clipping as they wear down quite well. I have seen pups kept on shingle, but immediately noticed how damp it seemed, and that the pups' feet were not hardened up as one would wish. Also, it is very hard to clean up quickly and efficiently with any of these loose surfaces. This is a subject on which everyone has their own pet theories, so I can only speak from my own personal experience.

As long as the shed or kennel is dry and weatherproof, there should be little need for any sort of heating except in extremely cold weather. If it is possible to line the inside walls, this helps considerably and also reduces the risk of draughts. Where prevailing weather conditions involve damp cold, I would be inclined to invest in a canine infra-red heater of the dull-emitter type. Dry cold is not so harmful as the damp. A slightly raised wooden bed with wooden 'walls' around is not a bad thing to have in the kennel, preferably with an opening to get in, away from the direct draught that will come through the door. These dog beds can usually be seen on the kennel manufacturers' stands at most of the big shows, but any home handyman can soon knock up something quite suitable for far less money!

House training is a big item to everyone, not least the dog himself! From the time that you get your puppy home, make sure that there is some newspaper down on the floor of the room where he will first be kept. Our puppies have plenty of newspaper on the floor from birth, and so are quite used to doing puddles on this surface. You need to be persistent for the first few days, until the 'message' has penetrated, and then the lesson is soon learned. Pick the pup up frequently and take it outside, telling him to 'puddle' or whatever word you use to make him understand what you are requiring. It is essential that you decide on *one* word and keep to it. When the required puddle has been produced, make a great fuss of the puppy so that he understands how pleased you are. Unexpected puddles can happen at times of excitement, so don't expose the pup to strangers, visitors, etc., without an extra little trip outside, even if the last one was only a few minutes before. First thing in the morning, before the whole family are about and moving around upstairs, slip down quickly and quietly and put the pup out – it's amazing how many people expect him to last out through a period of noise from up above.

For the first few nights, we leave the whole of the kitchen floor covered with newspaper. In this way you find that by gradually leaving less and less, the odd puddle will usually be on the remaining piece of paper rather than on the surrounding floor. When the paper has been left dry for perhaps a week, then it should be safe to assume that you have a reliable dog. This may sound a massive operation, but will be quickly accomplished if you do not flag at any time or depart from routine. Our first Bobtail was house-trained within three weeks, and slept upstairs for the rest of his life. If one of our puppies goes to a family, I always tell the mother to remember how she toilet-trained the children, and to adopt roughly the same principles with the puppy, even though the practical details may be somewhat different!

Car training is another thing which is best started early. Our pups have a ride round the block before a meal, and soon get used to the motion of the car. If you take them out too soon after a meal the disturbance can make them sick. Make sure the puppy is comfortable, and not likely to fall off the seat or suffer anything frightening. Several short drives are best in the early stages, and then the car soon becomes a familiar place. A dog which is reluctant to go in a car can sometimes be helped by sitting in the stationary vehicle in order to get used to the different surroundings. Sit there with him, make a fuss of him, and he will soon overcome his fear. Any young dog can become suddenly excited, and for reasons of safety I strongly advise fitting a dog guard to protect the driver from the sudden onslaught of a boisterous puppy. If there is anyone in the back to restrain him, then all may be well, but so many of us travel alone, and in these circumstances I would not take a youngster out without a guard. It has happened that a dog has dived out through the driver's open window, with disastrous consequences.

As your dog becomes used to travelling, longer journeys can be made without any worry, and many show dogs make trips of hundreds of miles each week with no trouble at all. Do make sure that the ventilation in the car is sufficient for the dog's comfort; they soon become very hot and start panting when there is little or no air circulating. Besides their discomfort, excessive panting can lead to drooling and very wet, messy beards, most undesirable when on the way to a show!

Basic obedience is easily established in the home. 'No' is the first word to be understood, and the tone in which it is used is most important. Any sort of laughter in the voice at the time of correction is to be deprecated. A puppy cannot understand if one day he is corrected sternly, while the next his misdeeds are treated as amusing. 'Sit', 'Stay' and 'Come' are other commands which are best learned early on. When saying 'Sit', a little gentle pressure may be put upon the rump, so that the action of sitting down is associated with this command. After a little patient practice, this instruction will be very quickly obeyed.

'Stay' is not quite so easy to teach, as a friendly pup will want to follow when you take a few steps back. Here I would suggest that having got him into the sitting position, you only take a step or two back to start with, and keep saying 'Stay' in a firm voice. I usually show the flat of my hand, with the fingers pointing upwards, so that later on even the hand action can be taken as the command without the need to speak. Bobtails learn quickly, so it will not be long before 'Stay' is understood too.

When he has learned to stay, the word 'Come' can be called in a friendly, encouraging tone, so that he will understand that this cancels out the previous command. Some people will want to get their puppy trained very quickly, but here again remember that puppies are very similar to young children, whose interest can soon wane, so keep the obedience lessons short and end them with some fuss and show of affection, so that the pupil understands you are pleased with his efforts even if they are not always perfect! The last thing you must do is to show any signs of temper, as this can undo any good work already accomplished. Learning to walk on collar and lead comes under basic obedience too. Don't suddenly put collar and lead on a youngster and expect to have a perfectly man-nered dog trotting alongside you. The first move is to put the collar on for just a few moments, so that the unfamiliar feeling of something around the neck is experienced briefly. Then take it off, and tell him what a good boy he has been. Gradually increase the time that the collar is left on, and then try to lead for just a few steps. He will most probably want to go in a dif-ferent direction from you, so gently pull him in the way you have decided, without any sharp jerking. It will need a little patience, but the pup soon learns that he goes in the direction that *you* decide!

The training required for the show ring is easy once you have accustomed him to the basic commands which we have just discussed. Walking, trotting and possibly galloping are the types of movement usually required by the judge, and these are all better if done on a loose lead so that the animal is not pulled too close to the handler. The ability to stand still for a period and be handled by a stranger is also very necessary in the show dog. Standing for a short while, and then being praised for being so good, is the best way to start, then gradually extend the time from a few seconds to maybe a couple of minutes and he will soon get the idea. To be willingly examined by a stranger *without* attempting to jump up and play, is essential! If you have friends or neighbours who will co-operate in this, ask them to run their hands over the pup in the manner of a show judge, and to examine closely the points that will be noted in the ring. Looking at eyes, teeth and mouth, plus the actual handling of the muzzle, head, etc., are all part of good training. If your local Canine Society has classes for show-ring schooling these are invaluable, as they attempt to reproduce the atmosphere of the show. It is not authentic, of course, but taking part in a line-up of other dogs, being handled in turn, made to stand, and then to move, are all things which will be part of those frequent show days which will roll along in the future.

Bobtails are a very perceptive breed, and can almost read one's thoughts, I find. They soon understand if they are doing something wrong, and are also delighted when they realize that they have been very good and are deserving of praise. There are naturally times when correction is necessary, and this should always be treated in a serious manner as I mentioned previously. It is useless to be cross with them for doing something one day, and then the next day to laugh at the same thing; this only produces a bewildered puppy. Make sure that he understands when you are pleased, too. A few encouraging words soon reassure an uncertain youngster, just as firm, sharp tones indicate that he is in the wrong. Persistent naughtiness calls for firmer treatment, and I have found that Bobtails are like children in this respect and a sharp slap is best. I do not agree with the idea of perpetually waving a rolled-up newspaper at any dog, for this can lead ultimately to the animal taking such a dislike to it that every newspaper is attacked on sight! When a Bobtail has grown a good thick coat, nothing will penetrate its covering, so the most sensitive part is the nose. I *do not* mean that a great big thump is called for, but the quick slap is usually enough to remind him you are the boss and expect to be obeyed.

5

The Growing Animal

ONE very important feature in the growing puppy is the coat. When you collect your puppy, he has a short, black coat, and you may wonder how long it will be before the beautiful long blue coat appears. Signs of a change soon become apparent when the black puppy coat grows a little longer, and then in certain places some blue hairs can be seen. The usual places for this change to be first noticed are at the base of the neck and above the hocks. Then the coat gradually starts to change all over, and it is then that the most grooming must be carried out. From the time you first bring your puppy home, accustom him to the feel of the brush and comb, though more for him to get used to it than for actual grooming in the early stages. As the coat lengthens, the need to comb becomes more apparent, and while a brush can be used to give a flick-over to present a good appearance, there is nothing so effective as a thorough comb-through when the puppy coat needs to be moved.

If neglected the soft puppy coat can soon become balled-up and form into mats which are most unpleasant for the puppy, not at all nice for the owner to feel or see, and very difficult to remove. Regular removal of the dead puppy coat will leave the way clear for the new, adult coat to come through. The puppy coat is dead or dying when it becomes the colour of cocoa; brown tips are usually dead hair, and the sooner they are removed, the better. An experienced owner may feel inclined to hasten the departure of the puppy coat by pulling a lot of it out between finger and thumb, but you need to know what you are doing here, otherwise you will probably have a violent

protest from the sufferer! I have heard that the rubber finger-
stalls used by cashiers for note-counting are ideal for pulling
dead coat, but I have never tried it myself, preferring to use the
comb as much as possible at this stage.

Once the old coat has been removed, then the comb-
through can stop, and the comb will only be required for the
whiskers or the removal of any undiscovered matted lumps.
The new under-coat will now grow in, and the longer, outer
hair will also come into active growth. Sometimes the adult
coat comes through in a very pale silvery colour, but eventually darkens to a good blue shade with maturity. Again,
some adult coats are inclined to be rather patchy, but these
usually even out in the adult dog, or – to use the technical term
– they 'clear'.

Sometimes, for one reason or another, the puppy coat does
not receive the attention it requires, and the dead soft coat
then mats up into a rather unpleasant blanket. If this is allowed
to go on too long, the only remedy for the comfort and hygiene
of the animal is to carefully clip. It is indeed a great shame that
a dog should be allowed to get into such a state, but the sooner
a matted-up coat is removed, the quicker the new coat will be
able to grow in.

If you are keeping your Bobtail as a pet, with absolutely no
thoughts of exhibiting, then the coat is much easier to care for
if the under-coat is kept to a minimum. Few people have the
time to give a very thorough brushing at frequent intervals, so
if a once-weekly comb-through is possible, the thicker under-
coat will never become too profuse with the consequent mat-
ting. Then all that is needed each day is a quick check to ensure
that eyes and bottom are clean, and a brush-up to make your
pet look glamorous. Should the show ring be your aim,
however, you will need to do all you can to preserve the adult's
beautifully thick under-coat, or at least encourage it to grow in.
Here the grooming takes on a different aspect, and time and
patience are required. Provided the puppy has been taught to
stand from very early days, preferably on a table, the chore is
made so much easier.

Once he will confidently stand on a table, get him used to
lying on his side, but do not force this on him too soon as it is

essential that he feels completely secure at this elevated level. Part of the grooming routine is the same for both show and pet dogs. Check that eyes are clean, and free of the congealed mucus that so easily collects in a little ball at the corner. This is usually fairly firm, and can be lifted off, but if there is any sign of a running eye do watch this carefully, and remove the gummed-up mess with a piece of clean material soaked in some boiled warm water as a preliminary step.

Ears must also be regularly checked, for with the great amount of hair growing in and around them troubles can soon appear and multiply if not discovered and treated. I do not like the idea of pulling the hair out from the inside of the ear; we should feel intense pain ourselves, and so will dogs if this is done. When the dog is sitting quietly, without any distractions, I carefully clip the surplus hair out of the cavity. Any matted lumps can soon be very painful, and cause great soreness, so do watch this very carefully. I *never* put any form of powder into a dog's ear. If it needs more cleaning than a gentle wipe-out with a piece of cotton-wool, then a drop of slightly warmed olive oil should be used. Should there be any really unpleasant smell, don't hesitate to call on your vet's professional services, as any form of ear complaint can reduce a dog to a state of nervous frustration. The pain is naturally upsetting, and as they are unable to deal with it themselves they usually rub the affected side along any convenient piece of furniture, or else start to scratch with great vigour, thus causing further soreness. The trouble must be dealt with quickly, if it is anything apart from the normal wax which can be wiped out.

Teeth are often forgotten; they get dirty and coated with tartar just as ours do. There are several recommended ways of cleaning. A common one is to damp a rag, put some common salt on to it, and then rub over the teeth. Many people find our own toothpaste, in particular the special brands for smokers, are very good. Recently a canine toothpaste has come on to the market, and has been made available mainly on the trade stands at the shows. Very badly coated teeth will need to be dealt with professionally, and the vet will usually scale the offending matter away.

Feet are often neglected too. The hair which grows between the pads can get very long and thick, and if not regularly inspected will combine with mud and grit to form large balls of uncomfortable matter right in between the pads, with resulting soreness. I find the best way to keep feet clean and comfortable is to carefully clip away the hair, not *too* closely, but sufficient to discourage matting-up. Nails must be carefully checked too. A dog which gets plenty of exercise on hard surfaces will rarely need much attention apart from a little rub round with a file to tidy up any rough edges, but an animal which gets most of its exercise on soft, pliable surfaces, and grass, will usually grow nails longer than strictly desirable, and if not inspected and clipped back from time to time the long nails will affect movement. Puppy nails grow very quickly, and ours are regularly cut back from the age of three weeks. Long nails cause the pads to spread, thus losing the tight, firm foot.

Sometimes, in bad weather, pads may crack and dry, so this also needs watching; if found to be cracked, I use pure lanoline to soothe and heal the condition. Occasionally one finds that dew claws have not been removed, or that where the root has not been completely removed (at the time of tail-docking and dew-claw removal) one claw has grown again. This must be watched with care, and will need clipping back more frequently than the other nails. Nail-cutting on a dog should not be done with ordinary scissors, as these flatten the nail and make it split. Special nail clippers can be bought on the trade stands at most of the larger dog shows, or if you feel you cannot cope with the actual clipping yourself, your vet will do the job for you.

On most Bobtails, the nail is of pale greyish colour, in which you can easily see the pink quick growing inside. This must *never* be cut, as it will cause bleeding, so do use the clippers very carefully and ensure that they are correctly placed so that the quick is not damaged. On some dogs the nail may be black and here again great caution must be exercised.

Having checked over the various parts, we come to the actual grooming. There are several types of brush in popular use, and users of each will assure the novice that his or hers is the only correct one! If uncertain, you would be wise to consult your breeder or local Bobtail enthusiast. I would never advocate going into a local pet store and being persuaded that the most expensive brush they have in stock is the very best! One of the most popular types with Bobtail owners cost about 30p in the old days, and can still be purchased fairly cheaply. Many breeders will only use a whalebone brush, but these are very expensive and often difficult to obtain. The Mason Pearson type of human hairbrush is also in use, in increasing numbers.

With the dog laid on its side, I find it easier to brush *away* from my own body, so that I am leaning over the dog. Others may find that they can get on better by brushing towards themselves. I normally start with the hair on the shoulders, just above the leg, and brush out in a line along the body. When one line is done, I go up a little higher until the top of the back is reached. Turning the dog over on to the other side, I repeat the procedure. With the sides of the body done, I then do the stomach, taking great care to check that there are no matted lumps under the arm-pits. The front is best done in two halves, or alternatively you may care to have the dog stand up, and then do the whole front of the chest and up under the chin in one stage.

Once the body has been tidied up, I go on to the legs, checking that there are no matted areas in between the toes on the top of the foot; if there are, and these are allowed to remain, they soon become very thick and discoloured, often a nasty red colour. After body and legs, we come to the head. Take care to see that no tangles are left around the ears, on the cheeks or around the beard. Here, a comb may be necessary to tease out some of the knots, but it should be dealt with piece by piece and gently teased out, not tugged at so that the whole lump of hair is wrenched out.

Having given a good overall grooming, stand the dog up and proceed to brush the coat in the following way: From between the ears, up to the nose, brush the head hair forward, so as to give the effect of a large chrysanthemum. The hair on the neck, front and shoulders should then be brushed down, whilst that on the legs (at the front) is brushed up. If you find that brushing up the legs disturbs the hair on the shoulders, this should be flicked down, as the general effect must be one of straightness in front. Brush down the neck hair over the shoulders and on to the back, then place your hand here, at the top of the shoulder, while you brush the hair which is further down the back up towards the head. This applies to that right over the rump, and all on the legs. Looking down on the body from above, one should get the impression of a pear shape.

Figure 10   Pear-shaped – from above

Now you have a beautifully groomed Bobtail which you will want to take out for a walk. As long as all the injections for immunization are completed, a little stroll will do no harm provided the puppy is quite used to the feel of the collar, and won't be constantly trying to slip it off. I never buy a very expensive collar for a growing Bobtail, as they increase in size so fast that it can be a very expensive proposition. If you have several puppies in succession, as a breeder might, then it is probably more economical in the long run to have a dearer collar for use at each stage of growth.

To the one-dog owner, I would recommend buying a strong but fairly inexpensive leather collar, which will need to be replaced after perhaps three or four months. When the Bobtail is fully grown, it is a good investment to purchase a collar made of rolled leather, with flattened ends. The rolled collar does not rub and pull on the coat so much as a flat one will. *Never* use a chain choke collar, or for that matter a leather choke collar, as they pull the hair through the ring as they tighten, and a rather sparse neck covering will soon result.

When exercising a young pup, a lightweight lead is best, being fairly long so that the pup can be allowed some distance to run when conditions permit. This long lead will be very helpful when you are training him to come back to you at your command. A gentle pull on the lead indicates your command to 'Come', and means exactly what the lead is doing – pulling him back to you. When you have an obedient dog, and no longer need such a long length of lead, you will be able to get a shorter, stronger type. Many people prefer one of round, plaited leather, with a flat hand-piece. This type is very strong, and not so hard on your fingers if you have to pull the dog in close to you with some force.

Now we have dealt with grooming and feeding, we must think of playthings. Most puppies are given a multitude of these, but end up with one or two favourites. In our house, the first thing to be taken over was my husband's slippers. So, if you want to avoid the ruination of a perfectly good pair of slippers, try to find a substitute first! An old pair of leather shoes, with any buckles or trimmings removed, is always acceptable for a good quiet chew. Some rubber toys are made especially for dogs, but they must be quite strong and fairly large, as the capacity of a Bobtail pup's mouth has to be seen to be believed! A piece of middle marrow bone is good to chew on. I ask the butcher to chop the ends, and divide the long tube part into about three sections. These can then be baked carefully in the oven, to get the marrow soft, or gently simmered in a saucepan. I remove the marrow, and use it a little at a time in a meat meal. I do not like to give a pup too much marrow at a time, as in my experience I have found it tended to loosen the stomach. A marrow bone will give endless hours of pleasure, and will often be carted around the house as an inseparable companion!

Since this book was first written, supplies of fresh meat have not been so plentiful and, in common with many owners, I have taken to using a 'complete' food, having tried and tested several, in the form of either pellets or meal. To the meals the owner may add canned meat, tripe etc., while the others are a complete food in themselves. Many of these complete foods can be fed either dry or soaked for a specified period in warm water. Those that can be treated in this manner are usually termed 'expanded'. When feeding complete foods, in dried form, the dog will naturally drink more, so it is essential that ample fresh, clean water is always available. I still wean my puppies as previously stated, putting them on to complete food when about ten to twelve weeks old.

6

Breeding

Preparations and mating

POSSESSION of a bitch does not necessarily mean that you must breed from her; similarly, no owner of a dog should feel that he must be used at stud. Naturally, if one has a good specimen, the next logical step is to consider attempting to perpetuate the blood-line. It should normally be safe to assume that a good show specimen is also structurally sound, but this should be checked before attempting to breed. When the animal was bought as a puppy, you obviously tried to pick out a healthy specimen that was as sound as possible, and if your breeder was careful the parents were certified clear of any signs of hip dysplasia. Now, if *you* are to breed, it is your turn to get the hips checked, and this can be done by using a tranquilliser or under general anaesthetic and – with the dog completely relaxed – the X-rays can be taken in the manner prescribed by the veterinary authorities. Some vets do not have the necessary equipment, in which case they may be able to recommend you to a neighbouring colleague, or even to the nearest veterinary college or veterinary research station where the apparatus is of the most efficient type.

After you have received a certificate stating that there is no sign of hip dysplasia, ask the vet to check that there is no deafness or sign of entropion, cataract, or PRA. Once he is satisfied on all these counts, you have cleared a big hurdle. If, at any stage of the investigation, he is not happy on any of these points, ask him about seeking a second opinion. Should there be only a small margin of doubt, he will probably be willing to do this, but if he finds definite evidence of any hereditary defect, then *please* do not think of breeding from the animal and perpetuating a fault.

Sometimes a novice owner is very keen to have an early litter from a bitch, but should be firmly discouraged from considering this until the bitch is on her third season or is at least 18–20 months old. The breeding of puppies from bitches on their first season is not unknown, but is very much to be deplored. Any stud-dog owner has the right to refuse a stud if not satisfied that the bitch is old enough, and he should also ask to see certificates of clearance from hereditary defects. If the bitch's owner is unwilling to produce such a clearance, signed by a qualified veterinary practitioner, then suspicion will naturally arise that perhaps the bitch is unsound. So often, the dog is blamed for throwing faulty stock, and the owner of the bitch concerned is unwilling to admit that it takes two to make the fault, so the dog's owner must do everything possible to safeguard his dog's name. One parent clear of hereditary defects is not sufficient to guarantee a healthy, sound litter, so both owners are equally responsible in this respect. The choice of sire and dam must be carefully made: it is not good enough to rush over to somebody in the next town or village because they are willing to let your Bobtail mate with theirs of the opposite sex. If the study of a pedigree is completely beyond an owner, he should not be too proud to seek the advice of someone long established in the breed who has a knowledge of the lines and can give helpful advice.

There are points in favour of line-breeding, whilst others are of the firm opinion that to strengthen up a breed completely outcrossing is the only answer. With the perpetual shadow of hereditary defects in the back of one's mind, it is essential that if any form of close-breeding is contemplated one should take into account the weaknesses which will be accentuated in addition to the points one is hoping to 'fix'. If the former outweigh the latter, then surely it is not a very clever gamble? There are also risks attached to combining two completely strange bloodlines, as there is no way of anticipating what will result. Most breeders are willing to tell the owner of their stock what they consider would be a good match, and the novice owner would do well to heed the advice of the expert.

Having made up your mind to breed from your precious bitch, it is assumed that you will have had her checked over and be quite happy that she is old enough and sufficiently fit to bear the anticipated litter. The stud dog to which she will be mated may well be quite a distance away, so preparations for the trip must be made, bearing in mind that bitches do not become ready for mating at the weekends only! Around the time that she is due in season, she should be checked carefully every day, and when she shows that she is truly on heat must be kept away from any males you have yourself or which could get in to visit. I do not believe that every bitch is ready for mating from her tenth or twelfth day. Each one has her own set day on which she is ready, and until one has been able to ascertain this great care must be taken to ensure that she is neither left too late for mating nor forced to submit to a union for which she is unready. A good stud dog will certainly not show any interest if the day is wrong. An over-sexed dog, however, will probably attempt a mating whether or not the time is right; if this is allowed, it could well be that at any subsequent mating the bitch will remember being forced to what was little short of rape, and be quite unwilling and thus upset a good stud.

A maiden bitch should be introduced to the male at about the tenth day, just to see if she is willing and he is interested. It may be that she is ready for an early mating, but if they are both disinterested they should be kept apart and the introduction repeated the following day. The fact that a bitch is losing quite heavily, and still showing a strong colour, does not imply that the time is wrong. I had a bitch who was ready on her fourteenth day, and then continued to show strong colour for almost another week after the mating. Productive matings have been carried out as late as the eighteenth or twentieth day of heat, but this is uncommon. A mating is usually more prolific if it takes place later rather than earlier in the season, as the ova (or eggs) are shed over a period of time, and the more that are down and ready for fertilization, the greater the chance of a good-sized litter. If the stud dog lives far away, then it is sometimes impracticable for daily visits to take place, so every other day may be necessary.

Some owners of stud dogs have accommodation where visiting bitches can be kept quite safely, with no fear of their escaping. If such an arrangement is made in your case, take the bitch there a few days before it is anticipated that she will be ready for mating, to give her a chance to settle down and become relaxed after her journey. If she has a favourite piece of bedding or plaything, then take it with her for comfort. Where the owner of the dog is keen that your good quality bitch should be mated to his stud, the prospect of keeping her for perhaps a week or ten days will be readily accepted. A stud fee covers the mating alone, so you must expect to pay for the keep of your bitch while she is staying there. Some owners make it plain that their stud fee includes up to a certain length of time of attention whilst waiting for the correct day, but do not assume that everyone adopts this arrangement. If you ask beforehand, then it can be satisfactorily settled without any embarrassment.

If you are lucky enough to be within easy reach of the chosen stud dog, then the mating process is so much easier. Allow the bitch time to relax after the car trip, and let her have a run to relieve herself, if she wishes. When she is relaxed and ready, then gently introduce the pair to each other, with the owners holding their respective animals by collar and lead if any temperament is expected. If no leads are used, it is always advisable for both animals to wear good strong collars in case a situation arises when they need firm handling. Some stud dogs are not inclined to waste any time, and will attempt to mount the bitch without any real courtship, while others like to prance around and maybe circle her a few times before attempting to proceed with the mating. *Never, ever* force a dog to mount a bitch, as it will put him off other matings. He will possibly need some help, especially if he and the bitch are not quite compatible for size. As long as he attempts to penetrate her, he can be carefully handled, without any haste, to guide him right into the bitch. If he has not been handled from the very start of his stud career he will not be used to accepting help, and may refuse to go any further if a difficult mating comes along.

Patience should be the watchword at a mating, with no sign of haste; this is a natural animal function, and cannot be controlled with one eye on the clock. If, after some attempts, both animals seem tired, separate them and leave for a rest, before bringing them together again a little later. They are more likely to try to mate if in a quiet and secluded place without a lot of spectators present. Should the bitch be a maiden (i.e. has never been bred from), she may be harder to mate, either from fear or just nervousness; in these circumstances she may need to be held, not only in position, but from underneath to prevent her from sitting down each time the dog mounts her. If she is very strong or self-willed, it may even be necessary for two people to hold her, in addition to a third person attending to the dog. Successful penetration will result in what is called the 'tie' in almost all cases, although there are occasional exceptions.

Although the dog's organ is quite large and stiff before actually entering the bitch, it enlarges even more after penetrating her, at which time the very swollen part near the base is held firmly by the bitch's contracting to a certain extent. It is during this period of being firmly joined together that the conception takes place. Sometimes there is no 'tie', and it is doubtful whether conception has occurred, for the fluid containing the sperms flows out at the rear of the bitch and is lost. If a bitch is known to be unable to hold a dog which has penetrated her, they should be held together for a while, if possible for as long as eight to ten minutes. With a normal mating, once the pair are perfectly happily tied, the front and one rear leg of the dog should be carefully lifted over the back of the bitch, to one side, so that they are standing end to end. This is known as 'turning', and some experienced dogs will do it of their own accord as soon as they are ready. On no account should they be left alone at this stage; if the bitch is getting tired or bored, she may attempt to sit down, and this could result in serious injury to either or both of them. The dog may also attempt to make some vigorous movement after the tie takes place, and this again could be the cause of injury.

After being held still for some time (maybe only a few

minutes or perhaps as long as twenty minutes), the pair will part quite naturally, as the dog's penis subsides to a more normal size, and the bitch releases her hold on his organ. Once they are parted, they should be taken away from each other. The dog should be gently wiped down with a very mild antiseptic solution of a non-irritant nature, and if the sheath over the penis is still stretched back this should be gently eased into place with a little vaseline or similar soothing cream. The bitch should be restrained from any exercise for a while, and if possible kept fairly closely confined for an hour or so before she is allowed to urinate. Whatever happens, don't load her up into the car and start off on a hectic journey home. At least two hours' rest is necessary to allow her to calm down completely, and a night's rest is even better. Some owners feel that their bitch should have two matings, but if the first was of good duration, and in every respect appeared satisfactory, then something like several million sperms will have been released. Little would be achieved by a second coupling, therefore, unless an interval of two or three days between allows time for more eggs to be released.

A disadvantage of two matings some days apart lies in the theory that puppies can be conceived at each mating, involving either a prolonged whelping for the bitch or premature birth of the puppies from the later mating which might therefore be of a weakly nature. The number of pups in a litter is mainly influenced by the dam, since only eggs which have been released can be fertilized. A sterile male, or one of low fertility, can be the cause of poor litters, but this would soon be apparent as the dog would consistently fail to throw larger litters. Sometimes a bitch and dog may have what seems to be a perfect mating, yet nothing results from it. If the bitch goes to other fertile studs with the same lack of success, then it could be that she has an acid vagina, and will probably conceive if douched out with an alkaline solution before the next mating. Bicarbonate of soda is the most popular ingredient for douching, which I would advise is done by a veterinary surgeon. The reproductive parts are in a sensitive state already, and it would not be wise to clumsily attempt to douche her out and so upset her that she resists any attempts on the dog's part to mate her.

An owner who has watched, and helped the vet to douche a bitch, may feel confident enough to undertake subsequent douches unaided, but great care must always be taken to be as gentle as possible.

The welfare of the stud is most important. It is impossible to expect him to be a keen stud and fully fertile if he is not treated with thought and consideration. Ample exercise will keep him in hard condition, whereas lack of exercise will make him fat, lazy, and sluggish when it comes to sex. Only the best of food is good enough for him, and it must contain the essential vitamins to encourage the production of sperm, i.e. vitamins A, B and E. A young dog who appears to be very keen can be used about once a week over a limited period. Ideally, however, once every three or four weeks is best for him, giving him a chance to regain his vigour and potency with a good interval between bitches. To use a young dog too often can easily result in complete loss of fertility.

Whelping

When the bitch has been returned home, don't suddenly treat her as a complete invalid, depriving her of normal routine exercise and possibly overfeeding her. Mine are treated quite normally, except that I add bone flour to the meat meal at night, together with fish liver oil in capsule form. After three or four weeks, an increased appetite becomes apparent, when the meat ration should be increased together with extra eggs, cheese, milk or other high-protein foods. Try to avoid any undue increase in starch intake, as she will not want to be carrying surplus fat. After six weeks, I give two feeds per day, increasing to three feeds for the last ten days. I have never yet known a Bobtail bitch go to her full term of gestation, which is recognized as sixty-three days, so it is well to ensure that she is not left unattended for the last week of her pregnancy. The usual sign that the whelping process is getting started is that she goes off her food and starts passing all the solids from her stomach. Towards the end she will probably appear to be very loose, but this is nothing to worry about.

In preparing for this time, ensure that she is quite clean

about her body, and that any hair surrounding her vulva and around the nipples has been removed. I always clip all over the stomach, as with the long coat of a Bobtail the hair can become knotted and form a noose for the tiny puppies; it is not unknown for a dead puppy to be found, hanging in its mother's profuse coat. Near to the time of whelping, the stomach and rear should be carefully washed with some sort of disinfectant, but this must *not* contain carbolic which is poisonous. By taking these precautions you can ensure that all is as clean as possible when the puppies come nuzzling around looking for food.

Some time before the whelping is due, you should have decided where the event will take place, put the whelping box there and encouraged the bitch to go in and out of it, and also to sleep in it. If she shows any reluctance to go into the box, try getting into it yourself, with her meal. She will be happier to see that you regard it as a good place to be, and the fact that her food is there should be sufficient encouragement. Bobtail litters can be as numerous as ten or even more, so do ensure that the box is large enough for her to lie stretched right out, with ample room for the puppies to lie all around her without getting squashed. An overhang, on the lines of a pig farrowing place, is a good idea, as the boards or rods prevent her from lying hard up against the sides of the box and thus allow the pups to wriggle along the edge without having her roll over on to them. The box should be scrubbed out with mild disinfectant such as Dettol or something similar, and the floor covered closely all over with many layers of newspaper. As the whelping progresses, it is thus possible to tear off any soiled areas of the paper, leaving her undisturbed and with plenty still underneath her.

When the emptying of the stomach seems to be completed, it is usually noticeable that her breathing has become slightly faster, and that she is panting quite a bit. This is the time to get her into the whelping box, for very soon things will start to happen!

One does not wish to anticipate trouble, but it is always well to keep in touch with the vet when a whelping is imminent.

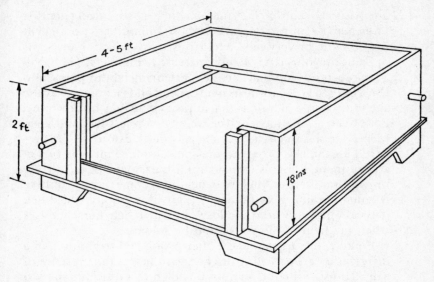

Figure 11   Whelping box
Raised off floor; large and strong. Allow enough room
for bitch to lie on her side and stretch out. Box will
probably need to be 4 feet to 5 feet square. Rails pre-
vent whelps being crushed against box-side by bitch.
Three or four tongued and grooved floorboards can
close entrance as whelps grow active.

Mine calls to see the prospective mother, and gives her a
check-over, about a week before she is due to whelp. She then
knows him if he is called in for emergency reasons. I telephone
at the onset of whelping to inform him, and he either leaves a
number where he can be contacted if away from home or surgery, or alternatively can phone in every few hours if he is very
mobile. Unless you have reason to expect difficulties, there is
no real advantage in asking him to come as whelping starts, for
common sense is what is most needed at that time. You may be
lucky enough to be able to call on the help of a friend who is
experienced in such events, and most particularly is known

and trusted by the bitch. A maiden bitch who is having her first litter may begin to panic when these unfamiliar experiences begin, so do be very calm and firmly reassuring, for any signs of panic on your part will only increase her anxiety. There will be some indication that she is experiencing labour pains, and she will keep going towards her rear end and cleaning away the slight discharge of mucus that appears. She may lie down in a fairly relaxed manner, or she may be very restless and keep turning round in circles. As she gets more disturbed, be prepared for the first puppy to make its entrance into the box at any moment. Bobtails are usually fairly easy whelpers, and one or two strains are enough to expel the average puppy. If there is much straining without any sign of a puppy, the bitch naturally gets very tired and loses the will to help herself; this is when the help of the vet should be sought.

Equally, the appearance – after prolonged straining – of a dirty, rather evil-smelling discharge, indicates the presence of a dead puppy, and the vet must be called very quickly if the rest of the litter are to be born safely. The normal puppy emerges from its mother in a bag made of membrane. Sometimes this bag is burst as the pup arrives and the head appears before it is right out of the dam's body, whilst others may be quite tightly sealed up inside. It is essential that the bag should be broken open without any delay, and the owner may have to show an inexperienced bitch how to do this if she seems unable to understand what is happening.

After being shown how to deal with the first few, she will probably be happy to take over this part by herself; in so doing, and cleaning the puppy, she will also devour each bag. As the pup is born, you will see that it is attached to the dam by a thin cord; this is the umbilical cord through which it has received sustenance while in the womb. This cord must be cut, and an experienced bitch will nip it neatly with her teeth. If she is unwilling to do this, or does not seem to know what is necessary, then the owner must cut it with *sterile* scissors. An impatient bitch will not nip the cord carefully, but may pull and tug at it which, being the common cause of umbilical hernias, should be avoided if at all possible.

Once the pup is severed from the dam, she should proceed to lick it quite vigorously, which not only cleans it but encourages its circulation and breathing. If she will not do this, again the owner has to step in and help. First, make certain that the mouth and nose are clear of any tacky mucus which could be inhaled with sad results, and then gently rub the puppy with a piece of old, worn towel. A maiden bitch is really like a child at school, and needs to be taught what to do, so after showing her how to deal with the first one or two babies, give her the chance to get on with the job herself, but do watch to see that she does not either panic or lose interest. Should the puppies be born very quickly, then she will need all your help, for as fast as one is being cleaned up and encouraged to breathe another is likely to be in the process of birth.

Always keep a check on the time during a whelping. Make a note of the time vigorous straining commences, and if it continues for more than three hours without results the vet should be called. So long as puppies start to arrive within the three hours, then all is proceeding normally. Write down the time of each birth, and also if the bag is there. If there is no bag, note when it does appear later, or if it seems that there may be a bag left inside her the vet should be informed. Some owners like to put down the details and sex of the puppies, so that later they can look back and see how each one has progressed from birth. It is not uncommon to weigh puppies either, although this is something that I have never done myself. I don't think a bitch should be bothered at such an emotional time by having her pups handled unnecessarily. If you do decide that you want to weigh them, handle them very carefully and place them on a soft pad of towel or something similar, in the scales pan.

Sometimes what appears to be a dead puppy is born, but the owner should not give up without trying to bring it to life. Depressing the tongue and gently blowing down the throat a few times will sometimes bring about the desired result. Others find it helpful to move the front legs back and forth to encourage movements of the chest. The method I have used with some success is 'swinging'. Wrap the pup in warm towelling, hold it firmly about the body and – with feet wide apart – swing from above your head, down towards the floor. This has the effect of ridding the body of any excesses of liquid that may be in the lungs. While you are trying to help such a puppy, don't forget that the bitch is probably continuing to have more pups, and that she may still need assistance.

From the appearance of the first puppy at the start of whelping, until the arrival of what appears to be the last one, I find there is usually an average of about forty-five minutes between each. When you think the whelping process is finally completed, phone your vet to come and give the bitch a check-over. My vet always gives an injection of pituitrin to ensure that all the afterbirth is expelled plus an addition to the injection of broad-spectrum, anti-biotic. A further injection of calcium is also required. If there are any puppies which for reasons of deformity, etc., should not be kept, let him take them away and put them down painlessly. This must be done away from the mother, and she should not even see him take them away.

When the whelping is over, and the bitch is willing, take her out for a while to enable her to relieve herself. If one of you can do this, the other has a chance to get the whelping box cleared up, and any soiled paper removed, so that the mother returns to a clean, dry place, ready to settle down and suckle her babies. It is unlikely that she will want to eat anything for a while, but will welcome a good drink of some proprietary brand of canine milk. During the whelping she may have been able to take some small drinks, but after it is all over she will enjoy being given a little extra attention. Add some glucose to the milk; we use a tablespoon to a pint of liquid.

I have assumed that the bitch will be happy to have the newly-born puppies in the box whilst she is giving birth to the rest of the family, but some do not like this, in which case it is best to remove each cleaned puppy to a warmed box, where there is some soft material in which they can snuggle. Keep them fairly near to the whelping box, so that the mother can see them and is not worried that you have taken them away.

Post-natal

Bobtail puppies are born with smooth, black coats, and a tail of quite generous length. The coat begins to fluff out a bit as they grow, but is rarely of a blue shade at this early age. Where there are white markings, they are there for life, the only exception being the odd white hairs that may show in the body coat and which tend to disappear as the coat grows and eventually changes colour.

The bitch will soon gain a good appetite, and with a litter to feed she must have food at regular intervals and of the very best quality, for it is from this that she will draw the nourishment to pass on to her offspring. I give best beef (to which are added multivitamins, iron, calcium, etc., all of which she will need in ample quantity once a day), and to this I add raw eggs. To drink she has Supergold, which for rearing a big litter can be bought most economically in the breeders' pack. At this stage I don't use biscuit meal at all. The bitch's stomach remains quite loose for some time, as she is not only eating herself but cleaning up all the waste from the puppies, so it is inevitable that her tummy will not return to normal working for quite a while. Don't attempt to stop her from cleaning the pups by doing it for her, as this is a natural process for both parent and offspring. The gentle licking around the stomach and rear end of each puppy helps the digestive system and bowels to work, and should not be interfered with. Only if a bitch will not do this must the owner try to act as a substitute by gently massaging the stomach with a rag or flannel which has been wrung out in fairly warm water. If the stomach is not encouraged to work properly, then the puppy will feel quite full and not be interested in feeding, and if not remedied, in time this can mean his gradual decline.

While it is essential that the bitch be allowed to whelp quietly without too much noise and spectators, it is equally important that as soon as the litter start to take an interest in what goes on around them they should be allowed to become familiar with the sights and sounds of normal everyday life. Our pups have the radio left on from first thing in the morning until bedtime, so all the sounds from that are familiar. They should not be handled at a very early age, although this is what everyone wants to do, but they will soon be accustomed to all the members of the family. I don't normally allow anyone to disturb the peace until they are well over the tail-docking, have their eyes open and are trying to walk about. For the first few days after birth, all that is necessary is that they should be kept warm, well fed, and that the bitch cleans them.

No later than the fourth day, docking should be done. Most owners prefer that their veterinary surgeon should do this, as the best method is to stitch down the little flap of skin that is left. Some of the older breeders do their own tail-docking with apparent success, but I must admit that I do like to know that there are stitches to hold everything together, and that it will not be so easily opened up by the bitch when cleaning. The stitches usually remain in for about 5–7 days, and when removed there is a neat little patch which should cause no trouble at all. These days, we tie tails with rubber bands instead of cutting them off. About four days later they come off quite cleanly and very close to the body in a very satisfactory manner. It is not fair to expect the bitch to be unmoved at tail-docking times, so do arrange for her to be right away from the scene when this is done. Some owners find that they can get the mother out for a walk, others that if she is a car-addict they can take her for a ride. Give the vet plenty of time to do the job, and make sure that they are all back in the whelping box, clean and tidy, before the mother sees them again. They will doubtless be very hungry by then, so if she is kept busy feeding them the chances are that she will not be too upset. There is a theory that Bobtails have become a tail-less breed after many generations, and that they should therefore be born without tails, but this is only a very rare occurrence as with any other breed.

So long as you are giving the bitch ample food, and the puppies are like little hamsters, then all is well provided that she has enough milk and nipples to cope with them all. Should the litter be very large, it will be necessary to supplement her feeding. Most chemists stock the special feeding bottles for premature babies, made by John Bell and Croyden, but if you have an emergency, an eye-dropper is enough to carry on with until the right thing can be obtained. The aforementioned Supergold is claimed to be an excellent substitute for bitch's milk, and I must say that I have used it with very satisfactory results. With a goodly sized litter, there is every hope that the bitch can cope with them for the first three weeks, but if they are not doing as well as hoped it may be worth trying to wean them earlier. There seem to be two schools of thought on the best way to wean. Some advocate raw scraped meat as the first taste after mother's milk, but I use human baby weaning cereal, mixed to a semi-liquid state; since they are used to milk, this does not feel very much different. To the cereal I add some glucose for extra strength, which I feel at this stage of early weaning is all that is necessary since they should be getting minerals, vitamins and calcium from the dam. If by any chance this does not seem to be the case, then consult your vet as to the best additive which will not upset such tiny stomachs. As puppies can take so much out of their dam, it is advisable to give her a further calcium injection ten days after whelping. Calcium shortage in the bitch is known as 'eclampsia', and, if ignored, can be serious. Signs of disinterest, restlessness, snappiness or other uncharacteristic behaviour should make one suspect eclampsia and the vet be called immediately.

It is hopeless to expect puppies to lap straight away from a dish, and invariably some, or all of them, will attempt to wade into it! We take each puppy individually, carefully wrap a towel around the shoulders enclosing the front legs (so that they don't try to get into the saucer), and with the puppy tucked under one arm gently dip the tip of its nose in the cereal. The feel of something unfamiliar will cause it to lick the strange substance away, and so if you make sure that the liquid in the dish can be easily reached they will usually try to lick at that too. They get the idea almost immediately, and are quite eager to clear it up.

To start with, we give no more than a tablespoon of the mixture. Be prepared to clean each puppy carefully but firmly, since quite a lot of the cereal will go in places other than the mouth! While the towel should keep some of the gummy food off, there is often quite a lot around the face and head. We find the easiest plan is to have a bowl of warm water at the ready, plus a flannel, so that immediately after the feed the puppy can be gently cleaned, dried and put somewhere safely until the rest are fed. If you have a fairly deep-sided box, with sufficient floor area, put in something soft for them to lie on, and by separating them you will have no difficulty in sorting out which have been fed and which are still waiting. If any cereal is left over, we usually let the dam have it, and she feels just as pampered as her babes! With the whole family fed, they can be returned to the whelping box once you have ensured that it, too, is clean and sweet; mother will probably give them all a quick lick over, and proceed to let them have a drink of her milk before they go off to sleep.

Although they have started weaning, this does not mean that you should immediately start to cut back on the dam's rations. As the puppies grow, so the amount of milk they will want to suckle is greater, and therefore she should still be fed in a generous manner. I find that the best time to give the weaning meal is at about 9.30 in the morning, when the family are out of the way and the job can be tackled without any distractions. It is a fairly slow business to start with, and may occupy the best part of the morning until they get the idea; at this point they can soon have an individual dish down on the floor and get on with it themselves.

If you can have some help with the first few weaning feeds it makes your task so much easier, just as it helps to have some-one else around when you first let them free to eat from dishes. I have recollections of little 'paddi-paws' sploshing all through cereal and back out again on the newspaper! This feed should be repeated at tea-time. After they have become used to cereal, which takes about four days, I add to it some liquidized meat, first at one of the meals, then at both. In this way, I find that the little stomachs become accustomed to meat without too much upset.

When this routine has been established, and they are obviously ready for the next step, you can proceed to a proper meat meal. This should be made up of finely minced meat, to which is added an egg plus some sort of roughage. I normally

First feed

Body shape revealed by clipping

Ch Oakhill Peter Pan

Ch Pendlefold Prince
Hal
(*C. M. Cooke*)

Ch Pendlefold Sweet
Charity of
Cinderwood

Bobbie Blue

(*Diane Pearce*)

Ch Farleydene Fezziwig

Ch Aberfells Georgy
Porgy, holder of
record number of
CCs
(*Jeff Curd*)

Don Carlos pictured
at 15 months, on
winning his first
Challenge Certificate
(*Diane Pearce*)

Ch Jedforest Don
Carlos, May 1983,
Supreme Best in Show
at Scottish Kennel
Club with owner/
breeder Mrs Jean
Collins
John Hartley/Our Dogs

mix in some Farex, which makes it drier than the cereal/meat combination, so if you find that they are not so ready to accept this moisten it with a little broth or meat juice, put small lumps on your finger-tip and gently put into their mouths. Once they have it in the mouth they find that it is not so bad after all, and should soon get used to this next new thing. However keen they are to feed, don't overdo the quantities given to start with; a level tablespoon of solid or semi-solid food is plenty in the beginning. The owner may feel inclined to feed the puppies with extra amounts when she sees how eager they are, but this only leads to digestive troubles and loose, upset stomachs.

At about this time the teeth should begin to come through, and the dam will start to show some reluctance to feed her family. This is very understandable, as the teeth are needle-sharp and soon make her nipples sore. When it becomes apparent that they do not need mother's milk so much, start to give drinks of Supergold canine milk, and only put them to the dam for a short while to draw off any surplus that she may have. Do *not* suddenly stop her feeding them, unless of course her milk completely dries up of its own accord, as this can lead to trouble. If her milk does not gradually diminish, then you may have to seek your vet's help. When making up milk for puppies, do ensure that it is not too hot, but it must be slightly warmed as this is how they are accustomed to drinking it from the mother. To each pint of milk, once a day I add one raw egg which is whipped up smoothly into the mixture, together with a dessertspoon of powdered glucose.

Independence

I find that my puppies are ready to finish suckling from the mother at about three to four weeks of age, and suggest the following diet at that time:

Early morning: feed of milk with the egg and glucose, with some Farex or Farley's Rusks broken up and mixed in.

Late morning: minced meat, preferably raw, moistened with broth or gravy, into which is stirred some fine puppy meal which thus becomes moist all over.

Mid-afternoon: milk with cereal.

Early evening: repeat of the late morning meal.

Supper: last thing at night is a milky, thickened feed, but not too thick.

As I said previously, the meat meal can be thickened with some sort of cereal, and when they are able to take it this can be changed for puppy meal. As an interim additive to the meat feed, I find it very satisfactory to bridge the changeover from Farex to puppy meal, with a wheatmeal milled very much more finely than the latter. All the solid meals should be followed by a milk drink, but don't give the milk beforehand since the pups will then feel fairly full before beginning to take their solid food. Daily additives should be fish-liver oil and calcium; either cod or halibut liver oil can be used, and I find the most satisfactory form of calcium is steamed bone flour.

At eight weeks of age, it is possible to cut the meals to four per day, feeding milk and meat meals alternately so that they get two of each. I keep up the four-meals-daily routine until twelve weeks of age, when three meals per day are usually found to be sufficient. These should be a cereal breakfast, meat lunch, maybe a little milk at teatime, and then a main meat meal in the evening. At six months they are usually happy to go on to two meals per day, with a cereal and milk breakfast and a meat supper. As they grow larger, the baby cereal foods can be dropped in favour of human cereals such as rice crispies, cornflakes, etc. Try not to choose those with much roughage, as the other canine foods will give sufficient bulk to the digestive system. The additives should be continued all through the period of growth; in fact I keep these up until they are some fifteen months old, as well as giving fish liver oil to all stock during the winter.

Once the dam has finished feeding the litter, there is no need to continue the calcium for her, but I do keep up the fish liver oil and extra eggs in order to help her build up her strength. I find it easiest to give a growing puppy its daily dosage of fish liver oil by capsule, one per day. The bone flour is given at the rate of a teaspoon for weaned pups, increasing to a dessertspoon at ten weeks, three teaspoons at sixteen weeks, a tablespoon at six months, three dessertspoons at eight months, finally increasing to two tablespoons daily from ten months until growth is completed. Any excess will not be likely to cause harm, as the body will eliminate it. Some breeders like to use veterinary yeast, while others prefer seaweed powder or Cytacon in liquid or tablet form. This is just a case of personal preference – there seems little to choose between them.

Emergency preparations

We have dealt with what is assumed to be a normal litter, all the puppies wanting to feed in a straightforward manner and not causing any anxiety. Luckily, most litters are like this, but one should always be prepared in case any problems arise. Sometimes the actual whelping may be a long and exhausting process during which the bitch loses all interest in her family, and should it be a very harrowing experience she may well refuse to have anything to do with the babies. If she is weak, it may take her some time to regain strength, and in the meantime the pups must not be allowed to fade.

If a foster-mother is to hand, much worry can be avoided, but all too often there is a time lag between the call for a foster and her actual appearance. When you have found her, take care not to force the puppies on to her too quickly, but give her time to accept them calmly, if possible in semi-darkness so that she is not quite so aware of the difference. By morning they will have adopted her smell, and there should be little more trouble; it is only during the first few hours that she should be watched. In an emergency, I have heard of very much smaller breeds accepting the odd Bobtail pup and rearing it quite successfully. In fact, one breeder had a pup of some six ounces, which was successfully reared by one of her miniature dachshunds.

If no outside help is available with rearing, then hand-feeding every two hours round the clock is the only answer. The box in which the litter is kept should be in a very warm place, with no variations in temperature. Make sure that no cold air can seep up from underneath the box, and if you have hot-water bottles available put one or more under a blanket, taking care that they are not too hot. See that the box is shielded from any draughts, and that it cannot get damp. Goat's milk – if available – is preferable to that of cows, but I come down heavily in favour of Evenlode's Supergold, which has been specially formulated and balanced for just such a need. Glucose is an important additive here, plus a few drops of fish-liver oil added daily to one of the feeds.

I have already mentioned the premature-baby feeder, but until one can be found the eye-dropper is better than nothing. Don't try to force the milk into the pups too quickly; a drop at a time is all that they can comfortably take. If you try to get them to feed too fast, they will only choke. Take care to check that each puppy has a satisfactory bowel action, for it will soon be disastrous if the bowels become clogged up. The stomach and rear end of the puppy should be very gently massaged to encourage bowel actions, both after each feed and before the next. If there are signs that the pups are not making the required progress, your vet may let you have a quantity of liquid protein which will produce results almost immediately; he will give you directions as to the amount to use. I have used this very successfully on a tiny bitch which did not seem to be keeping up with the rest of her litter.

Growing up and hardening off

All too soon the puppies, which opened their eyes at about 10–14 days, will be feeling their feet and starting to wobble their early steps in the box, and even sooner it will be seen that they need more room. If the box is so designed that some boards can be taken out at the front entrance, the puppies will start to stagger out on to the floor. Try to have the litter in a room where the floor can be thoroughly scrubbed and then covered in quantities of newspaper, so that the clearing-up will be fairly easy.

Each time they are let out for a walk around, the ample floor protection will mean that it is simple to tear off any soiled pieces of the paper and place them in a box or sack for subsequent burning. From the time of birth, you should keep the puppies as warm and draught-free as possible, keeping a dull-emitting infra-red lamp burning continuously if the room heating is insufficient. When the puppies attempt to get about on their own, they begin to generate their own body warmth, and do not need to be perpetually under the lamp. This can then be turned off in the day, as long as the room temperature does not drop as well, and switched on again at night. Make sure that the lamp is suspended quite safely above the box, so that if the dam stands up it is well above her back. If it is too close to the puppies, it will cause dehydration. Proper insulation is an essential safeguard. Should it be necessary to have the litter outside all the time, then it will be more used there than indoors, except in really warm summer weather when it will only be on at night.

Some breeders find that they can keep a litter indoors until the time comes for the pups to venture outside the box. If they are kept in the family living-room or kitchen, the thought of having a busy little mob all around one's feet is not so appealing at this stage! The change from the house to the outside accommodation should be carefully planned and carried out. Make sure that there is no damp in the living quarters, and that they are quite draught-proof. Some form of night heating must be available, and if the weather is not very warm, it should be turned on in the day as well. Oil heaters are not considered 100% safe, since they can be tipped over or even begin to smoke and soot up a place very quickly, possibly causing the suffocation of young stock in such a closed atmosphere. Electric heaters can be very good, but do make certain that any wires are not within chewing reach of busy little pups. The wires should be suspended above, with particular regard for proper insulation.

If the weather is cold, damp or windy, don't try to get the puppies outside for a while, as they can soon catch a chill. A small run inside the outdoor kennel or shed is safer at this stage of hardening them up. When there is sunny, dry weather, try them outside for a short while, gradually lengthening the time they are allowed out. If they should get damp, do be quite certain that they are dried off before being put back in the shed or kennel. The dam will most probably want to visit her flock at certain times, and may still be inclined to give them a quick clean-up, but most of the time she will be happy to leave them undisturbed. They will still regard her as the source of milk, and if they can get under her will sometimes make an attempt to get some milk, much to her discomfort.

When the litter is about 5½ weeks old, I give them their first worming dose. Using tablets from the veterinary surgeon, they are dosed at the same time as their dam, with a repeat dose in about 10–12 days. It is often a great shock to a novice breeder to see just how badly infested a litter can become. This should not be regarded as anything but normal, however, and any excreta should be quickly removed before the pups can start to nose around the droppings. The modern vermifuge is so much more convenient than those of days gone by, when the custom was to starve off the dogs before worming. Nowadays, this is not necessary at all, the dose being mixed into each individual's food. The second dosing should not be neglected, because the vermifuge stuns the worms so that they will not resist and are expelled in a motion. They can, however, leave behind any eggs they have laid, and these in turn will hatch out, so they must be removed by the second dosing before they can become large enough to start the whole reproductive cycle all over again. It is known that lice are the host of worm eggs, and so care must always be taken to ensure that all stock is kept quite free of every sort of vermin.

If a bitch has to be treated for vermin just prior to having a litter, take your vet's advice as to which powder or spray to use, as it must be of a safe type; any residue could otherwise be taken by the pups from the dam's coat with disastrous results. As lice are to be carefully looked for and destroyed, always remember that straw is also known to be a carrier of lice, so no bedding should be made of this material. If newspaper is not enough, and you feel that some sort of material is required, use something which can be easily and frequently washed. In these modern times, when so many households have a washing machine, blankets of the ex-service type can be quite usefully employed as bedding. I do not like any wood shavings or sawdust, since the origin of this is sometimes dubious, and wood wool can cause eye irritations if it happens to get rubbed against the tiny eyes. To my mind, clean newspaper cannot be bettered, as it is cheap, easily come by and just as easy to dispose of. The dog-owner who also breeds soon gets the word around to family and friends, and in no time at all he is the recipient of all the surplus newspapers that can be used. We are the dropping-off point for several households, and have never run out, for from the time of the whelping until after the litter are all away, it is quite astonishing just how much paper a few puppies can get through!

In recent years we have seen the advent of a synthetic fur fabric which is easily washed and dried. This is popular as bedding for it is very warm as well as providing an easy surface for whelps to stand and walk on.

Grading and selling

I think we have covered the main points with regard to raising a litter. There are several very good books dealing exclusively with breeding, whelping and rearing, and the keen owner would do well to obtain a copy of one of these for greater technical detail on the various aspects than I can possibly provide here.

By the time the litter is well and truly established and the pups on their way to becoming adults, the owner has had ample time to observe them as specimens of the breed. After a while, certain youngsters tend to stand out for qualities which they possess over and above their siblings, and you may find that you are thinking in terms of grading them. If there is an experienced breeder of some years' standing living nearby, find out if he is willing to let you have the benefit of his advice. Often, the owner of the original stud dog will be sufficiently interested to want to come and see the progeny, and may also be anxious to try to pick out the best specimens.

If you all agree on what seem to be the best youngsters, who are of good shape and conformation, well balanced and with no obvious faults, you will probably decide that they should go to homes where – if they continue to show their early promise – they may eventually go into the show ring. One would be very lucky if every single whelp showed great promise and ended up as a show dog, but every breeder lives in hopes! The puppy which shows any fault which would make it unsuitable for an owner to show, can become the much-loved pet of some happy family, and give many years of pleasure and companionship. Grading must be carried out very carefully, for your reputation as a breeder of quality and integrity depends on the stock you sell for show and which actually enters the show ring. It is better to turn down a sale if you are unable to supply a puppy to fill a particular order, than to get rid of an unsuitable specimen because it happens to be available.

When picking out a puppy for showing, this is still quite a gamble at, say, eight weeks of age, but there are certain points that you can check, and if any of them are not up to standard at this age, it would be foolish to rate such a pup as a show prospect. A nice wide-skulled, rather square head is to be desired; eyes dark, or wall-eyed; mouth should at this age be tending to the overshot position rather than dead level, as so often a mouth which is level at eight weeks will end up as undershot later. One cannot have great hopes of any pup that is undershot at eight weeks; it may correct a little, but is unlikely to become perfect. There should be a good reach of neck apparent, even at this early age, and the front legs should be quite straight and in no way bandy. The back should be nice and short, with the signs of a good rise over the loin. The angulation of the hind legs should be visible, and they should – when viewed from the rear – be quite straight and not cow-

hocked or bowed out. The tail should be removed, with no
stump visible, for if it is noticeable at this age there is a risk that
it may grow on a little. The puppy should be lively and full of
beans, with clear eyes and no discharges from eyes or nose.
The coat should be clear in colour, and shiny in appearance.
No puppy with an abnormal temperature or any sort of
stomach upset should be sold.

It is in the interests of the breeder, as well as those of the
purchaser, if the vet gives it an inspection and issues a certificate of good health. Pricing is a debatable matter at the time of
writing, and there does not seem to be a scale of charges. Pet
prices can still be remarkably low – especially if the breeder is
keen for the dog to go to a particularly desirable permanent
home. On the other hand, especially good showing and breeding specimens can fetch several hundred pounds.

Having taken care to raise a fine litter, the important thing is
to decide who should have one of these precious little bundles.
Frequently one knows people who have seen and admired
one's bitch and who have waited patiently, often for up to a
year or more, to give a good home to one of her puppies. If
they are very keen, they have probably kept in touch
throughout this period, and gleaned much information from
you. Sometimes the owner of the stud dog will have passed on
any enquiries received for stock sired by his dog. He may have
taken the trouble to check on the prospective owners, and you
can feel able to accept his word that these are reliable and
trustworthy.

If the prospective customers don't fall into either of these
categories, you need to do some checking up. If they are not
too far from you, make the effort to go over and see what the
situation is; try to decide whether they have the room and sufficient common sense to bring up a Bobtail successfully. Are
they out at work all day? If so, they are not likely to make the
sort of home that you want for your puppy. If you find a very
disorganized household, with a mother who seems to be at her
wit's end and unable to cope with a young family, you can hardly
expect her to have either the time or the patience to cope with
yet another addition. These are the sort of points to bear in

mind. Should you feel that a Bobtail is wanted in order to impress the neighbours, with no thoughts of being able to cope with a very profuse adult coat, try to persuade them to find an easier breed to own. If you go into the matter carefully, and have doubts about the prospective owner's ability to cope successfully with a Bobtail, then it is far better to tell them tactfully but firmly that you don't think this breed is for them, than to have them appear on your doorstep in some months' time, saying that they do not want the dog any more. This is not scare-mongering, but has happened with sad regularity in recent times. The Bobtail Rescue Scheme would not be landed with so much work in such a short time if only more care were taken in the first place to ensure that the home is suitable for coping with and bringing up one of this breed.

Once you have visited your prospective owner, and found that all is quite satisfactory, then do make sure that they in turn come to see you, so that they can see a fully-grown animal and get some idea of what they are taking on. If they too are happy, then you can tell them many things that they will be eager to know.

Before any puppy of yours goes to a new owner, it is your turn to pass on the essential information about comprehensive diet and general care which you received when buying your original puppy. Set down a full diet programme from the time they collect the puppy (or it is sent to them) until it is fully grown, plus advice on worming, vaccination, collar and lead training, exercising, house-training, grooming and so on. Here is a rough layout for a simple diet and care sheet:

1   Feeding, including the types of meat to use, plus all the additives, etc. Give quantities at every stage of growth.
2   Bones and playthings.
3   Worming, vaccination, etc.
4   Collar and lead training. Exercise.
5   Suitable sleeping quarters.
6   House training.
7   Grooming, and choice of brush and comb.
8   Travel, and how to train for longer journeys.

9   Details of any helpful books which may be purchased.
10 Any points you think may be helpful regarding the
    individual pup concerned.

Some owners may get the chance to export from their litter.
Do remember that whatever is requested – a show or a pet
specimen – it is an advertisement for you and your breeding,
whatever grade you send. For this reason, I will not export anything that I rate as pet quality. In this country, we have a high
standard for our show ring, and anything less than the best will
be hard put to win more than moderately. Overseas, the standard is often really low, compared with ours, and an animal we
would consider to be of pet quality only can sometimes win
quite well, especially if the competition at that time is not very
strong. This may seem highly satisfactory, and the breeder is
delighted to hear of these wins, but the time may come when
the overseas owner wants to breed, and then finds that he has
not the nucleus which will enable him to produce stock of
great quality.

There is also the point, that other knowledgeable breeders,
seeing the poorer specimen, and assuming that it is typical of
the quality that particular breeder produces and sees fit to
export, will not bother to make enquiries about acquiring that
blood-line themselves. *Every export is an ambassador, not only of the
breed but of the breeder.* Some overseas owners arrange to come
and pick up their puppy, so that they can accompany it all the
way home, but others may not be in such fortunate circumstances and will have to have it shipped out to them. While
some breeders find that they can cope quite well with all the
forms, rules and regulations that accompany exporting, others
prefer to ask one of the established and reputable livestock
shippers to carry out the whole operation. This latter procedure is to be recommended for all those who are exporting
for the first time. Each puppy (or adult) that is exported
requires a Veterinary Health Certificate. Some countries have
specific requirements about blood tests, declarations, rabies
injections, etc., so it is as well to check on all these details either
through your vet, who will probably have the information

easily to hand, or direct with the Ministry of Agriculture at Tolworth, Surrey. Sometimes the foreign country's embassy is involved, so do allow plenty of time for all this paperwork to be completed.

If at all possible, send the puppy by direct airline flight into the nearest international airport, having agreed beforehand that it will be met on arrival. It is no good expecting a puppy to happily accept several changes of plane, etc., without getting disturbed. The size of travelling box is most important, and it must be large enough to allow the animal to stand up without the head being at all pressed down, and sufficiently wide for it to turn round without any difficulty. An old tea-chest with wire netting nailed over is *not* suitable for any travel, whether it be for a couple of hours or longer, yet people still expect stock to travel safely under such conditions. It is best if the top of the travel box is of a domed type, which ensures that no other boxes or freight can be stacked on top of it and allows air to circulate around. Make sure that there are plenty of air holes all round the box, and that the door is fastened securely in more than one place. The addition of several sheets of newspaper, fitting all over the floor of the box, will help to soak up any little puddle that may occur, and on top of this place an old piece of clean material or blanket which will not suffer if it becomes soiled. A familiar plaything in the box will add to the animal's feeling of security while on this long journey from familiar surroundings to a new home. Finally, if the puppy has eaten some time before the journey, and has had some exercise before being placed in the box, there is every hope that your overseas customer will open it to find a clean, sweet and lively puppy.

7

Shows and Showing

SOMETIMES the owner of a dog which has been intended purely as a pet decides to enter a small Exemption Show in the neighbourhood, and is delighted to be picked out among the prize-winners. This can be the start of a whole new way of life, and the making of many new friends both at home and abroad. Others have studied the breed with care, decided that they would like to show their dog, and have set out to buy a specimen that is likely to fulfil their ambitions. However carefully a breeder grades the litter, they can only be sold in the hope that each will continue to show the promise seen at eight weeks or so. No one in his right mind can guarantee that a very .young pup will turn out to be a certain Champion, and anyone who does make such a claim lays him/herself open to prosecution under the Trades Description Act if the dog does not come up to their promise. The conscientious breeder who realizes that you want something special, will most probably show you all the puppies available, and point out the reasons why some are better than others, for it is in his own interest that you should start off with the very best possible stock. If you take a good specimen into the show ring, then it is a living advertisement for a breeder of quality whose dogs come from sound blood-lines.

The training of a show dog starts from the time that you bring it home. In a previous chapter we have dealt with the need for any puppy to become used to standing and lying still while being groomed. Coupled with this start, I would stand the pup in the correct show position – if only for a few seconds at a time – so that it accepts this as part of life. Getting accustomed to the collar and lead is essential for every dog, and for the show dog the feel of the lighter-weight show lead will also be necessary. When the puppy is about five months old, it is worth finding out if your local canine society has training classes for ringcraft. There are usually such facilities within the reach of most people. If the only classes you can locate are for obedience, then this routine can be helpful, but do take care that your potential show dog is not trained to keep very close to your ankles (as in the obedience exercises) or that it is schooled to sit close to you every time you stop moving.

Some obedience clubs are very understanding about the requirements of the show dog, and will excuse him from certain parts of the exercises. Much of the training can be done at home, or when you are out walking: getting the youngster to walk or trot beside you, without pulling in all directions, should be a regular part of the training, and keeping the head up is absolutely essential. It is useless having a show dog that moves up and down the ring as if it were a vacuum cleaner, for it spoils the frontal appearance as well as the movement, and does not allow anyone to see the quality of neck and shoulders. If you have relatives and friends who are willing, ask them to run their hands over the puppy as if they were judging. The fact that they have not the slightest idea what a judge would be looking for is immaterial, so long as they can help the puppy to get used to anyone going over him at any time.

The grooming of the show dog is slightly more specialized in that the owner needs to take more care over certain aspects. Keeping the beard scrupulously clean is most important, since any stains will be apparent when the judge goes to look at teeth and mouth; do ensure, therefore, that if there has been a session of digging in the garden, or any other rather grubby occupation, all is washed off before the stain sets in! Make sure too that all the hair is allowed to grow naturally, without any of it being rubbed off by continual poking of the nose through gaps in a gate or fence.

The coat on the neck and shoulders usually grows to such an extent that it makes the Bobtail look rather woolly and thick at the front, so you may need to comb it out fairly regularly in

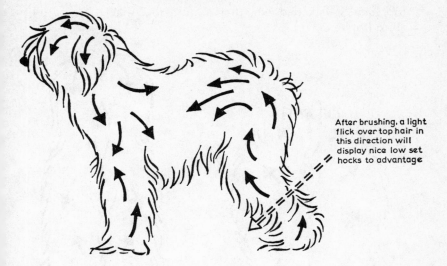

After brushing, a light
flick over top hair in
this direction will
display nice low set
hocks to advantage

Figure 12   Direction of brush strokes when grooming.
Hair will then fall into desired shape

order to show to advantage the good length of neck and the
nice straight front. The hair on face and head should be
brushed forward to give the appearance of one of those big
shaggy chrysanthemums, whilst that on the neck and
shoulders is brushed downwards. Brush the front legs hair up,
making sure that there is not an unsightly mess where that on
the shoulders comes down to meet it. If you brush up the legs
first, and then down the shoulders, it will give a good line. The
coat on the body should be brushed back just past the
shoulders in the direction of the tail; then that on the rear of
the body is brushed towards the rear, so that it stands up like a
giant powder-puff. If the hair on the back legs is long enough,
it can also be well brushed up to assume its more natural position, looking like a great pair of baggy pants. Viewed from
above, the body shape of the Bobtail should be like that of a
pear – narrow to the front, and wide at the rear. When the
(ideally) low-set hocks are first brushed upwards, and then the

top hair is flicked down, they should look like those of a shire horse.

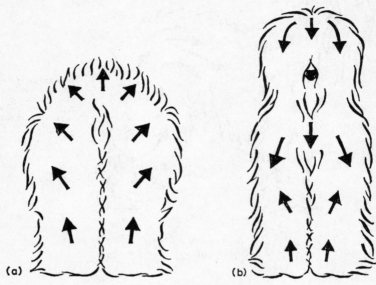

Figure 13   Brushing
(a) rear view, showing direction of brushing
(b) front view, indicating direction of brushing

Frequent bathing is to be deplored in normal circumstances. All that should be necessary if dirty, is that the white parts are washed out and dried off without too much rubbing in all directions. Use a good quality veterinary shampoo, taking care to rinse it all cleanly away afterwards. If find that J.D.S. Shampoo, marketed by the makers of Vetzyme, is ideal for Bobtails. If you feel that you must bath your dog, do get this done at least a week before the show, since washing makes the coat soft and the ideal harsh texture is not restored at all quickly. When the dog stands after the bath, dry the hair by gently towelling down in the natural direction of growth, as any vigorous rubbing makes it mat solidly like a blanket. The dog should have as much of the surplus moisture dried out as possible, and then be left to finish drying out in a warm, draught-free place. I find that newspaper is about the best floor covering if you have a wet Bobtail, and over this we put some old cotton bed-sheets to avoid any discoloration from the newsprint.

When the hair is almost dry, a little whitening powder can be rubbed in, as some coats tend to adopt a very yellowish shade when freshly washed. There are numerous proprietary brands of dog cleaning and whitening preparations, but many owners prefer to use ordinary precipitated chalk, or starch. The most important thing is that all the powder should be removed by vigorous brushing afterwards. The Kennel Club Rules for the preparation of dogs for exhibition state that whitening chalks may be used, but they *must* be removed by brushing before the exhibit is taken into the show ring. How many exhibitors abide by this rule, I wonder? One often sees a judge pat a dog, only to cause clouds of powder to emerge from the coat! There is also the mistaken idea that if a coat is slightly dark, to fill it with chalk will make it appear lighter. Any experienced judge soon notices such an attempt at deception.

Having made up your mind to start showing, the next question is *where?* Most exhibitors would agree that there is nothing like starting out at breed club level, where the show is confined to the one breed. There are often experienced people present, who are only too happy to help a novice owner, and if you are lucky enough the breeder of your puppy may not only be there but also eager to help you to get your exhibit into the ring in sparkling condition. You can find out when and where the various breed clubs hold their shows, by writing to the honorary secretaries for details. They should also be able to tell you what canine societies in their respective areas schedule classes for your breed at their shows. The weekly dog papers (*Our Dogs* or *Dog World*) have a show advertisements section, where they give the dates and venues of forthcoming shows together with the name, address and telephone number of the show secretary. If you wish to obtain further information, all you need to do is write or telephone and ask them to send you a schedule; this is really a plan of the show, giving details of the classes being put on, plus the scale of charges for entry and so on, times of opening, commencement of judging, and closing. There are many different levels of classes possible, and the schedule provides full explanations concerning each class.

Let us assume that your nearest breed club has a show coming up when your puppy has just turned six months, and this is to be his and your début in the ring. If you ask the show secretary to send you the details, you will find an entry form enclosed with the schedule. The information required on this form is easily supplied, for you have it all on the Kennel Club Registration Card or the Pedigree supplied by the breeder. You are asked to state the registered name of the dog, its sex, date of birth, breeder, sire and dam, and the classes you wish to enter. For a puppy starting its show career, the best classes are: Minor Puppy (for those aged 6–9 months); Puppy (6–12 months); possibly Maiden (never having won a first prize at any show, Puppy and Special Puppy classes excepted). Two or three classes are ample for a first venture. Make sure that the entry form, plus any required entry fees, is posted off in good time to be received by the Show Secretary before the closing date. Some clubs will send you an Exhibitor's Pass; others, due to the tremendous increase in postal charges, give them out at the entrance to the show.

It is important to allow enough time to make your journey to the show and groom your exhibit thoroughly before commencement. The Puppy classes are normally the first to be judged, so you do not wish to arrive late and be called into the ring unprepared. Try to arrange for someone more experienced in showing to go before you, so that you can see exactly what they do and what is expected of their exhibit. This will make it easier for you. The judge has a steward to shepherd the classes into the ring, and to hand out the ring numbers; this number corresponds to that allocated to you in the Show Catalogue, so it is a help to the steward if you can remember yours and tell him what it is. There are special pins for fixing ring numbers, but a good strong safety-pin will do just as well. Pin it where it will not get in your way if you need to bend over your exhibit, and where it will easily be seen by the judge and steward when they mark up their books at the conclusion of judging the class. Having been to a Club Show, it is hoped that you will have enjoyed it sufficiently to wish to go on to further exhibiting, and possibly support your local Canine Society at its shows. Not every society can schedule classes for our breed, even at one show per year, which means that if you wish to exhibit locally you must enter in 'Not Separately Classified' classes. You may find yourself mixed up with all different shapes and sizes of breeds without separate classes, but it can be great fun and a most enjoyable social outing.

The Kennel Club has two levels of Special Awards, at which every owner-exhibitor can aim. The first is called a Junior Warrant; to attain this, you need to gain twenty-five points before the dog is eighteen months old, so from the time it is old enough to show at about six months you have just one year in which to do this. Points are awarded at the rate of one for a first place in a breed class at an Open Show, or a Championship Show where there are no Challenge Certificates on offer in the breed, and three points for a win in a breed class at a Championship Show where there are CCs on offer for the breed. Thus, a really good run at two or three Championship Shows could soon get the points mounting up. When you have reached the grand total of twenty-five, write to the Kennel Club giving details of the claim, together with show dates and details of the class wins, and provided they agree with your claim you will receive the Certificate stating that your dog has won its Junior Warrant. The other awards, of more merit, are correctly known as Challenge Certificates but called CCs for short. They are allocated to each breed by the Kennel Club, based on entry figures at Championship Shows where CCs are on offer. Old English Sheepdog registrations zoomed up so fast that we now have the fullest possible allocation of CCs, with sets being offered at every General Championship Show. The Group Society, elevated to Championship level, received a Challenge Certificate for Bobtails, as have the Working Breeds Societies in Scotland and Wales. Ten of the active breed clubs have Championship Shows.

In order to be eligible to award CCs, the judge-elect (if not already approved by the Kennel Club) has to complete a form giving details of his/her breed experience, judging experience, etc. This form, if sanctioned by the Championship Show Committee, is then passed on to the Kennel Club for consideration by the Judges Sub-Committee. Once the latter's approval has been given, the fact is published in the *Kennel Gazette* which is the official monthly publication of the Club. If someone has already awarded CCs, they must still be approved by the Kennel Club for each appointment, but there is no call for a special form to be completed every time. All General and Group Championship Shows must be 'benched'. This means that each dog has its own division of a benching unit, where it must be chained up during the time spent at the show, unless it is being groomed, exercised, or actually exhibited in the ring.

Some Championship Shows are indoors, through the winter months, but the most pleasant are those held out of doors in the good weather, where the dogs seem much happier when moving in the grass with plenty of room. The actual benching is under the cover of marquees, which in the very hot sunny weather provide welcome shade for both dog and owner. There is also some wet-weather judging accommodation, in case the expected sun and heat does not materialize! The judge at a Championship Show can expect to see some of the cream of the breed, all hoping that he will decide they are the best of their sex on that day. When the classes have been judged, the unbeaten exhibits of first one sex, then the other, are called into the ring; from them, the judge picks the one considered to be the best of that sex, and also a runner-up. Best of Sex is awarded the Challenge Certificate, and the Reserve placing is also given a card stating the position (Reserve CC), so that if a winner should later be disqualified when the Kennel Club checks the results, there is an immediate upgrading for the Reserve. When the two CC winners have been decided, then the judge must state which is to be Best of Breed, and this is the one which goes forward to the Group judging together with all the others who were Best of Breed in their respective breeds within the Working Group. After all the Groups have been judged, the judge for Best in Show will go over the winners and make the decision as to which exhibit is the Supreme Best in Show.

Seen from the judge's angle, the dogs present an entirely different picture from that of the exhibitor. We are all personally convinced that *our* dog is the very best, and go to shows in the expectation that if we are lucky enough to have the type that appeals to the judge we may go home with a red prize card denoting the award of a first place. As we go about the country, showing our dogs, it is soon evident that some judges prefer one type to another, and so we make mental notes that certain judges are worth remembering because if they have shown a preference for our youngster, there is a good chance that they will still like it when it matures. I know some people will dispute the mention of differing types, but one only has to see the line-up at both Club and Championship Show level, to realize that we have sizes ranging from the small, very compact right up to the taller, rangier types. When a judge is selecting four or five dogs for awards in a class, it is often very hard for him to choose them all from one type; so often those which look very appealing when standing, just do not please sufficiently when moved. Therefore, bearing his ideal in mind, he will try to keep to a type, but soundness is a very essential factor in a working breed such as the Bobtail, and so the eventual line-up may not be so even as one would wish.

I know that it is very tempting to approach the judge after your classes are finished, but please do not worry until *all* the judging is over and – with the Best of Breed award made – there should be time to raise queries, seek advice and so on. If there has been a very large entry, and you have not been lucky enough to get a place, don't expect the judge to remember every detail about your exhibit; having pulled out the finalists in a class, notes will have been taken on these, but there is not enough time for this to be done for every single exhibit. Do not be discouraged if you have not been lucky enough to be pulled out amongst the winners. You must be prepared to go up and down at times, and who is to say that next time the placings may not be completely reversed! Until you have shown under a particular judge, you cannot tell whether he or she is going to like your type of Bobtail, so you must be willing to show and see what happens. Sometimes a novice owner seems very lucky in getting several prizes at his or her first few shows, so here the story is reversed – don't be too disappointed if after some good wins, you get a few shows where you are not in the cards. It happens to us all and we must be able to take the rough with the smooth.

From time to time a query arises as to how one becomes a judge. There is no set formula for this at the present time in Great Britain. Some breed clubs do give tuition to aspiring judges at special classes, but here you can only learn what the instructor tells you and it is still a question of whether the pupil has what it takes to make a good judge.

A good 'eye' for a dog is essential, and this is something which – in my humble opinion – you can neither learn from anyone else nor read up in any number of books. Some people are excellent at book-learning, but when it comes to putting this into practice they are completely lost as soon as they get into a show ring. Others, while unable to assimilate all that is written in reference books, may have a good eye and the practical knowledge that makes them into judges whose opinion is eagerly sought. The Kennel Club has looked into the question of Student Judges, but this is a complex problem and will not be easily or speedily resolved to the satisfaction of all the breed clubs in existence.

The best preparation for breed judging is to own some stock, show it, learn from experience what is good and what is undesirable in the breed, and find out all you can about the correct way to prepare and handle it in the show ring. When you have something sound enough to breed from, and subsequently breed a good litter or two, and watch them growing up, this is all part of the experience which you will be glad to have behind you when you are first invited to judge.

The most pleasant way to start judging, in my opinion, was within one's own breed clubs with only the one breed involved. Here you could make your decisions without all the distractions that arise at an all-breed show. Nowadays, it is more common to start judging at an All-Breeds Show, with

perhaps four or slightly more, breed classes. The Committee
of the Club that invites you to make your judging début will
have carefully discussed the question of your first attempt, but
they cannot of course know your personal feelings on the subject. Honesty and truthfulness are much to be commended,
and when you receive the invitation to officiate consider these
points carefully: do you feel that you know enough, and can be
sufficiently impartial, to give fair and unbiased decisions? To
judge with malice, or to accept because you feel that by refusing
to do so you will lose face amongst others in the breed, is just
not good enough. Never mind *who* should be on the other end
of the lead, can you honestly say that you would award them a
first place even though you dislike the owner or handler? It
could happen that someone has placed you and your exhibit
quite unfavourably in the past, but this does not mean that you
should do the same to them – so search your heart and decide
if you can be completely unaffected by personal prejudices.
We all get a fluttery, butterfly feeling in the stomach at some
time in the early stages, and this will probably happen to you
on the first few occasions when you find yourself alone in the
centre of what seems to be acres of ring. Don't let this fear deter
you from accepting, for if everyone was similarly affected then
there would be very few judges left! So, having looked into the
question thoroughly, you make up your mind whether to
accept or refuse. Whatever your decision, do have the courtesy
to write to the Secretary at the earliest possible date.

If you feel that your answer must be 'No', there is no need to
feel very awful about making such a decision, for you can only
be respected for your honesty if you feel that you cannot
possibly face such a task. If the reply is to be 'Yes', then – after
you have posted the acceptance – settle back when you have
the time and inclination, and study the Breed Standard. You
may find it helpful to read all you can, but for goodness' sake
don't rush up to every breeder you meet and ask what you
should do. We all, being human, love to give advice, and it can
soon be very confusing if it is all conflicting! Should there be
certain judges whom you admire, and they are to be judging in
your locality in the fairly near future, you may find it quite

informative to sit at their ringside after you have finished your exhibiting and see how they proceed. I have always found it possible to learn a lot from stewarding too; without inferring that you could learn to judge in this way, I feel that this kind of experience does give you an insight into certain aspects of the job.

In the letter of invitation, you will most probably be asked if you wish to claim any expenses. If you are to be put to great expense which you can ill afford to bear out of your own pocket, there is no disgrace in asking for a contribution towards your outgoings. It would be a sad day for any breed if the opinions of certain judges were not available because they did not feel they could ask for help towards their travelling expenses and so on. If, on the other hand, expenses are moderate and you can manage to absorb them, there are few clubs who will not be grateful to you for judging in an honorary capacity. On the day of the show, allow plenty of time for your journey so that the officials and exhibitors are not kept waiting and wondering where the judge has got to! On arrival, make yourself known to the Secretary, and then stay quietly away from the exhibitors until you are called.

In order to be able to enjoy your judging, you need to be both comfortably and suitably dressed. It is useless wearing unfamiliar or tight clothes so that every few minutes you feel uncomfortable or have to adjust your waistband etc. Lady judges should make certain that when they bend over to examine the exhibits, their skirts do not go up round the waist, nor are so tight that they fear a split. (These remarks apply also to exhibitors!) Heels on ladies' shoes are another consideration, low-heeled shoes being by far the most suitable and comfortable. Very high heels will tend to put you off balance, and if you are on grass they will sink into it in a very unfortunate manner. The exhibitor who wears high heels will not have proper control over her exhibit, for the balance is likely to be affected so much that if the dog strains against the lead she can be pulled over very easily. Remember that a dog show is a beauty show for the animals only, and the exhibitor is there to show the dog and not him or herself, so dress neatly and unobtrusively. If you are judging, you can choose clothes a little different from those you would wear as an exhibitor, but please bear in mind that you have a job of work to do and dress accordingly!

Having got into the ring ready to do your judging, the first class will be called in. The club will provide you with an experienced steward, so let him proceed with giving out the ring numbers and – if it is a mixed class – with sorting out all the dogs to one end of the line and all the bitches to the other. When they are all arranged and any absentees have been noted, you can begin. Assuming that there is plenty of room (and, if you are indoors, that the floor surface is not too slippery), you may wish the entry to circle the ring two or three times in order to loosen up. If outdoors, this is usually enjoyed by the dogs and also gives you a chance to gain confidence. When they are all standing again, point to the first in the line to come out towards you in the middle of the ring, where you will have plenty of space to go all around it and also be able to stand back and view the dog from different angles if you wish.

Having made a thorough examination, ask the exhibitor to move the dog. The most popular manner is in a triangle, dog and handler going away from you to the right at an angle of about 45 degrees, then turning to their left so that they go in a straight line, and left again on their return to the judge. This means that you can see the hind movement going away, the side movement, and then the front movement as they come back to you. If you are not satisfied, or the dog does not go well, ask them to repeat this. You are now in charge, and you must be quite satisfied that you have seen all you want at this stage. When this is satisfactorily completed, a brief 'thank you' is a pleasant way to dismiss them, when they usually go to the other end of the line of exhibits. If there are a great many entries, you may find that when you have gone over all those in one class, it is easier to arrive at your final decisions by retaining about six and excusing the rest. Should you wish to double-check on any points, feel the coat again, or even see any of them move for a second time, then there is nothing wrong in this.

At this juncture I feel that I must draw attention to the great need for judges, at all levels, to have more than a passing knowledge of the required conformation. If a dog is made right, then hopefully it will move in the called-for manner. The OES is not an easy breed to judge, but there is no excuse for lack of knowledge of the basic structure. Judges are sometimes judged themselves – by an often exceptionally knowledgeable ringside, and so often one sees evidence of really undesirable points being ignored – or not even being found! In recent times, we have all seen winners displaying poor fronts, lack of lung and heart room, straight stifles, hind feet turning right out in a 'Charlie Chaplin' manner, to name but a few of the more common omissions. Not only is it a bad day for a breed when unworthy winners go forward, but it shows the judge up for what he is – lacking in knowledge and/or ability.

When you have finished, the usual procedure is to place the winners from the left-hand side towards the right. After you have got them lined up, and are satisfied that this is your final placing, indicate the fact to your steward so that he can call out the numbers of the winners and hand out the prize cards. You also need to note the numbers yourself, and the show organizers provide a judging book for this purpose. Most of these books have a small space in which you can write out any notes on the dogs in order to be able to make up your critique on all the winners. If you can write shorthand, the space may be big enough, otherwise it is as well to bring a notebook or pad with you. I find the best type is bound with a spiral, so that the pages turn over easily. Where Limited Members Shows or Open Shows are concerned, often all the dog weeklies require is a critique on the first places, with a note of the second and third. However, for Championship Shows they ask for notes on the first two in each class.

When you have taken the necessary notes, thank the exhibitors and they can then leave the ring, whereupon you return to the table in the corner of the ring while the steward gets the next class assembled. All too soon you find that it is all over, and that you have judged your first show! It is as well to get your notes expanded into a critique as soon as possible after the show, while the facts are still fresh in your mind. One small reminder – when you are sufficiently advanced to be the judge in the middle of the ring, please don't forget what it was like to be a novice starting in the dog-showing game, and treat any such beginners with particular care and understanding. A little extra consideration goes a long way with the newcomer, just as it does with the very experienced exhibitors who equally deserve to be treated as carefully as the new folk. They may have been showing since before you were born, and it is a great compliment to you that they are asking for your opinion.

If the show which you are attending is being run on a strict time-schedule, do try to keep to any requested times that may be noted down for you. It is rare for a breed club show to be run in too much of a hurry, provided the time of starting is not delayed, but with an all-breed Open Show it may well be that someone else is booked to use the ring after you, and it is only fair to finish with the minimum of delay so that every breed has a good chance to get their Best of Breed into the judging for Best in Show. This also applies to most Championship Shows. If you are to follow another breed into the ring, do report to the Secretary as soon as you arrive, so that they know you are available if it proves necessary to start earlier than originally planned. Also, let your ring steward know where you will be if he wants to come and find you as soon as the earlier breed is completed. Ring stewards are hard-working people, who – like yourself – are at the show in a purely honorary capacity, so please remember to thank them for their help when you have finished and – if possible – take a note of name or names so that they can be mentioned when you write up your report.

To sum up, the good judge:

1 Replies promptly to the invitation to judge.
2 Arrives at the show in good time, and reports for duty on arrival.
3 Goes to the ring when called on to do so.
4 Treats everyone with courtesy, and proceeds with the judg-

ing in a fair manner, handling the dogs firmly but
without roughness.

5 Takes enough notes of the winners to be able to write a read-
able critique, which is then posted off promptly to the dog
papers for publication.

The good judge does not make a long list of faults which are
then printed in the papers for everyone to read and possibly
condemn the dog. Criticism must be constructive, giving a
balanced picture of the exhibits, so that those who were not
present at the show can get a mental impression of the winners. If you can acquit yourself in this way, then there is every
chance that you will be invited again!

8

Bobtails Abroad

HERE in the United Kingdom, one very often thinks of America when speaking of exports abroad, for the Americans have consistently imported good stock for many years, and the breed is now more numerous over there than here in the mother country. Before the last war the Old English Sheepdog was mainly concentrated in one part of the USA – the north-eastern side – but now it has spread all over the vast continent, reaching down into Mexico and right up into the frozen north.

The first Old English Sheepdog exported into America is recorded as having been purchased in 1885 by S. M. Cleaver of the Glencho Kennels of East Bethlehem, Pennsylvania, from M. H. Lowe of Wednesbury. This dog was called Bob, and was the first of the breed registered in America, his number being 3163 in the American Kennel Register of January 1886. Bob's breeder, date of birth and pedigree are unknown, but we know that he was first exhibited at Philadelphia in 1885, and it was stated by Mr Lowe that 'Bob's sire and dam can lick all creation driving sheep or cattle'. This same Glencho Kennel imported the first bitch into the country. One of Bob's own daughters out of a bitch called Gipsy, her name was Judith, born 26 October 1883, and her breeder was the well-known Dr G. C. Edwardes-Ker. From Judith and Bob the first American litter was bred, born on 11 November 1885, and one of the off-spring of this father/daughter breeding was a bitch called Dame Hester; she was the first owner-bred Old English Sheep-dog to be exhibited, making her show début in a Mid-West show at Milwaukee in 1886. There was, of course, no specific provision for the breed to be exhibited, so they had to go into what was then known as the variety class, today better known as the miscellaneous class. There were no regulations in those days governing the registration of dogs for exhibition, so there were many imported in succeeding years that were not officially recorded anywhere.

After the registration of the Glencho dogs mentioned above, there is no record of any others until the year 1898, although the imports continued in a small but steady number. In 1889 attention was drawn to the breed by the publication of an article in *Turf, Field and Farm*. Freeman Lloyd was commissioned to pen this contribution by a wealthy industrialist called William Wade, who came from Pittsburgh. Lloyd had written up the Breed Standard for the breed in England in 1885, which was later polished up by Dr Edwardes-Ker and has remained unchanged in most respects since then. It is practically the same on both sides of the Atlantic even today.

During the 1890s Thomas Terry and James Mortimer were the most prominent persons in importing; they were partners in raising livestock and dogs at their famous Long Island farm. Mortimer was not only knowledgeable about the Old English Sheepdog, but played an important part in the raising of pure-bred dogs in the United States. He was the first great all-rounder judge in America, and an acknowledged expert on all matters relating to canine raising. Terry was the first to register an Old English Sheepdog kennel prefix with the American Kennel Club when they first accepted the registration of kennels in 1896. Also registered in 1896 were Colonel A. B. Hilton's Woodlawn Park and Henry Jarrett's Wellesbourne kennel names. Most of the Terry/Mortimer stock was bred by Dr Edwardes-Ker, and obtained through Freeman Lloyd. Early winners from the Terry/Mortimer partnership were Hempstead Bob, Herdsman II and Lord Mayor.

The distinction for showing the first Old English Sheepdog at the Westminster Show (American equivalent to the British Cruft's) went to S. M. Cleaver in 1890, when the Show was held on 11–14 February at the American Institute Fair Building in

New York City. The judge was Reginald F. Mayhew, and he
had only two entries to run his eye over, a dog called Orson
and a bitch named Queen Vick. In 1893 Hempstead Bob was
shown at the American Pet Dog Club, and it was from this
show appearance that the incorrect theory arose that he was
the.first of the breed to be shown at Westminster. J. Pierpont
Morgan purchased Herdsman II in 1895, and he was the first
of many wealthy American fanciers who through the years
added the Old English Sheepdog to their kennels. Out of the
ten wealthiest families in the United States, all with fortunes in
excess of 100 million dollars, the Goulds, Vanderbilts,
Guggenheims and Harrimans all owned, bred and exhibited
the breed in the early nineteen-hundreds.

Other very wealthy families who kept Bobtails up to the time
of the Second World War were the Tyler Morses, Morris Kinney,
William A. Jamison, P. Hamilton Goodsell, and Mrs Lewis
Roesler Renner who was extremely well known. Since they
were all independently wealthy, they were able to spend vast
sums of money on importing the very best dogs available, and
such great names as Ch Shepton Hero, Ch Brentwood Hero,
Ch Night Rider and Ch Tip Top Weather were all allowed to
leave their English kennels despite being described as 'not for
sale' upon preliminary enquiry. All these top English winners
and producers made the Atlantic crossing in time, and
although no authenticated details of prices paid can be found,
rumour has it that ten thousand dollars or more was quite
probable!

The well-known Collie kennel of the Morgans incorporated
Old English Sheepdogs, and their early famous winner was
Gillie who won in 1899, 1900 and 1901. In 1899 Collies and
Sheepdogs were included in the same classification, and in fact
at the Collie Club of America Speciality Show in 1899 the first
three places in Open Dog went to Bobtails, much to the
annoyance of the Collie owners! The three winning dogs were
Sir Charles (R. H. Williams), Gillie (Morgan) and Sir
Ethelburg (Williams), and Williams' bitch Dame Elfrida was
placed in fourth position in the Open Bitch class at the same
show. The judge, Henry Jarrett, was known as an early Bobtail

fancier. When the dog Gillie was registered with the American Kennel Club in 1898, it was the first of the breed to be so registered since the Glencho dogs back in 1887.

Since those days a large number of Bobtails have been registered in America, although it is only since the outbreak of the Second World War that dogs have had to be registered in order to be eligible to compete in American shows. Gillie, bred in England by Mr Llewellyn, was born on 1 September 1896, and his background features two of the most important Bobtails of the late nineteenth century, Watch Boy and Wall-Eyed Bob.

King Kroonah	Watch Boy	Stracathro Bouncing Bob Nellie II
	Blue Rock	Sir Caradoc Nellie II
Queenie	Herdsman	Wall-Eyed Bob Newbridge Lassie
	Prue	Sir Cavendish Lady Grizzle

Gillie { King Kroonah, Queenie }

Watch Boy, with his son Young Watch, and in turn Young Watch's son, Stylish Boy, are credited with having had more impact on the breed than any other Bobtails of the nineteenth century. It is claimed that close on 98% of the Bobtails alive in the United States, British Isles and other parts of the world, can be traced back to these very influential dogs. The Tilley brothers were a great help to the American breeders who were getting established in the early nineteen-hundreds, when they

Above Int and Scand
Ch Rollingsea Honey
Bear
(*Marianne Erlandsson*)

'Loyalblu' Bobtails,
imported from Great
Britain, in the Jordans'
old London taxi

Int Chs Reeuwijk's
Charming
Masterpiece and
Reeuwijk's Honest
to Goodness

Danish Ch Some
Buddy Canadian
Ambassador
(*Rassmussen*)

Aus Ch Loakespark Sportsman with
Mrs Marie Kavanagh

(Gerald Foyle)

World Ch Loakespark Brandy Soda at 9 months

Am Ch Loyalblu
Hendihap

(*Diane Pearce*)

Five generations of bitches. G.G. Grandmother, Rollingsea Sunbeam;
G. Grandmother, Ch Twotrees Break O'Day; Grandmother, Arthurian
Belle Aurore at Loakespark; Mother, Arthurian Scarlet O'Hara from
Loakespark; Puppy, Loakespark Morning Glory

usually took a team of Bobtails from Shepton Mallet in Somerset over to the annual Westminster Show. The judge in those days was Freeman Lloyd. Stylish Boy, born on 4 September 1898 and bred by Mr Potts and Mr Shepherd, was a dog that the Tilleys considered to be their best at that time. He was extensively used at stud in England, and after being placed second in the Dog class by Freeman Lloyd was purchased – together with three bitches – by the theatrical personalities Charles Frohman and Charles B. Dillingham. It is reported that they paid ten thousand dollars for the four animals. Their Hidden Brook Farm Kennels at White Plains in Westchester County were devoted exclusively to Old English Sheepdogs, and were under the management of an Englishman called Jack Harrison. Other American kennels at that time were also managed by English staff, who were trusted to make purchases on behalf of their employers, decide upon matings, which dogs were to be shown and so on.

Just after Frohman and Dillingham acquired Stylish Boy, they experienced a very serious fire in their kennels, and gave him to Reginald C. Vanderbilt; he was the owner of Sandy Point Farm Kennels, where some very fine specimens were bred, and a programme of exhibiting was carried out which included Stylish Boy's son, Sandy Point Rags, who was extensively employed at stud. This dog was also shown very frequently, and was awarded Winners Dog at the Westminster Show in both 1905 and 1906, becoming the sixth Old English Sheepdog to be a full American Champion. Watch Boy and Young Watch had almost completely white heads, while Stylish Boy's head was entirely white. Freeman Lloyd and others who were great students of the breed credit Stylish Boy for fixing the tendency to all-white heads, and having been so widely used at stud in England before crossing the Atlantic, his influence extended to both countries.

Prior to 1910, no less than fifteen Bobtails gained their American Championship titles, including Stylish Boy himself, Ringlow's Sultan who was his half-brother out of Young Watch, and Rowsley Conquest, Dolly Gray and Kenvil Blinkers who were all sired by him.

The Tilley brothers took teams of dogs from Shepton Mallet to America in 1903 and 1904, and the late Miss Tilley recalled hearing from their old kennelman Fred Padfield (known affectionately to us all as 'Paddy') how her father would be taken down to Shepton Mallet Station (now closed) with the dogs, when he set off for Bristol docks as the first step on the journey across the Atlantic. The crossing took several weeks, and so was not to be lightly undertaken. After the 1903 show, the breed was sufficiently noticed for specimens to be acquired by several well-known socialite families in the New York area. In fact, the spectators watching the Old English Sheepdog judging at the 1904 show were so wealthy and of such great social standing that the judge – George Raper – was advised to take his time and make a good show of the judging for the sake of the famous audience! As Best Dog he chose Wilberforce, owned by the Steadmans, while the Best Bitch for the second year running was the Tilleys' Bouncing Lass. It was in 1904 that Mr H. Tilley established the Old English Sheepdog Club of America, and the founder members numbered ten, but the club counts its age from the year it was officially recognized by the American Kennel Club in 1905; it is one of the twenty-five oldest breed clubs in the States, and began issuing an illustrated year book as far back as 1906. If anyone possesses one of the original copies, this would surely be worth a small fortune today to a serious student of the breed. During the First World War more enthusiasts joined the club, and were its mainstay in the years preceding the Second World War, the peak period being from 1921 until 1929. The first Old English Sheepdog Speciality Show was organized in 1921, after which this event became a firm fixture in the Bobtail year. During the period of the depression in the nineteen-thirties, the breed club was also adversely affected, but a few devoted enthusiasts managed to keep a small number of dogs, and even contrived to continue in a very small way through the Second World War and to keep some blood-lines alive.

It may be of interest to describe the first of the Bobtails to become Champions in America from 1904 on. The first bitch was called Lady Stumpie, born on 30 June 1896, by the Mayor of Newport out of Czarina; owned by Mr & Mrs W. C. Eustis, she was bred by the Englishman, Dr Griffith-Lock. The first dog was Mrs L. Trowbridge-Martin's English-bred Potsford Bob, born in November 1897, by Lion out of Judy. It is notable that in those days the usual age for a Bobtail to finish its title was about four years old, unlike present times when one hears of very immature youngsters being credited with the title of Champion. Puppies and young stock were taken in to the show ring then, but rarely gained points until they were really mature, and it was not uncommon for animals of eight, nine and even ten years of age to gain their titles. One notable bitch, owned by P. Hamilton Goodsell, produced no less than thirty-five puppies before she gained her title. The Tilley brothers exported ten of the first fifteen American Champions, and of these they actually bred three themselves. In fact, only two of the first fifteen were *not* bred in England. The three Tilley-bred dogs were Crossroads Quality, Gray Towers Peggy, and Druid Content. One of those not bred in England was believed to have come from the first Canadian-bred litter, by Ch King Edward out of Sally Harkaway. Four of the Bobtails who gained their titles – Captain Rough Weather, Dolly Gray, Ringlow's Sultan and King Edward – were owned by James A. Garland of New York City and Rhode Island, who was introduced to the breed by Frohman and Dillingham and also by his Newport neighbour, Reginald Vanderbilt.

In 1905 and 1906 Garland became ambitious, and acquired stock from which to build up his breeding programme at his North Prudence End Kennels in Newport. He engaged as manager Arthur Merrill, who was not only very well-informed about the dogs on both sides of the Atlantic, but was also an acknowledged expert on the care of heavily-coated breeds and their preparation for the show ring. Although Merrill was very active in the kennels, Garland was also deeply involved personally, and made such decisions as he thought fit concerning his dogs; his sudden and unexpected death from pneumonia resulted in the eventual closure of the kennel, for although his wife tried to carry on for a year she gave it up in 1908. His daughter had a brief period with the breed in the late nineteen-twenties under the Shelterfield prefix, and she bred Shelterfield Furbelow, owned by P. Hamilton Goodsell, which was one of the only two bitches to go Best of Breed at an Old English Sheepdog Speciality. Mr Goodsell had more than sixty years' experience in the breed, yet considered Shelterfield Furbelow to be the finest Old English Sheepdog bitch and the strongest Bobtail in hindquarters in all that time. However the Shelterfield Kennel did not continue its association with the breed for very long, being mainly known as a strong force in the Sealyham breed.

From 1908 until 1918, the Beaver Brook Kennels of Mrs Tyler Morse were dominant in the United States, not only in the breed but also by virtue of their own all-breed competition. Wealthy Americans have always been attracted to the Bobtail, and Mrs Tyler Morse was certainly rich, for her father (one of New York's construction magnates) left her a fortune of over two million dollars when he died in the early 1890s. She married at seventeen, and her husband used her fortune to build up a real estate empire in and around New York City; unfortunately the marriage failed, but when this happened her husband paid over to her some six million dollars, which represented a tidy profit on the original sum!

About six months after the divorce, she married Tyler Morse; he had been interested in pure-bred dogs for several years, but she was the driving force in building up the Old English Sheepdogs. When she died at an early age from pneumonia, she left her estate to her husband (who was also an executor) with the proviso that if he ever re-married he would forfeit all claim to it. Her first husband was left $250,000 in lieu of any claim against the estate. Morse never married again, and when he died he left the kennel, buildings and grounds to his manager, Arthur Merrill, who had come to them from Garland's North Prudence End Kennels when these were disbanded in 1908. Merrill had the full backing of his employers, and the Morses spared no expense in setting him up with the finest possible stock and equipment. They imported the best they could obtain, and only acquired animals whose quality had already been proved in their own country. They not only purchased the best English stock direct, but also bought home-bred litters out of imported English animals.

At the great annual Westminster Show, the Bobtails were dominated for many years by the Morses' exhibits, which won in 1908, 1909, 1910, 1912, 1913, 1914, 1915, 1916, 1917 and 1918. In addition to all these Best of Breeds, their bitch Ch Slumber was Best in Show in 1914, and in 1915 their dog Ch Brentwood Hero was Reserve Best in Show, a success which Ch Slumber repeated in 1916. They imported more than twenty-five specimens from England, including Ch Shepton Hero and his son Ch Brentwood Hero who were the two top producing studs of their day. On first enquiry they were told that these dogs were not available for sale at any price, but both eventually ended up in the Beaver Brook Kennel. There is no record of the price paid, but it is said that Shepton Hero cost $3,000 in 1909 at the age of four, and his son cost a little less two years later. Shepton Hero, born on 24 March 1905, was bred by the Tilleys, by Lord Cedric out of Avalon Lass, and was Winners Dog at Westminster in 1910. His son Brentwood Hero was born on 22 April 1908, out of Ch Brentwood Country Girl. Both were noted winners and producers in their home country before being exported to America. Brentwood Hero was Winners Dog at Westminster in 1913, 1915 and again in 1918 when nearly ten years of age. In 1915 he was second Best in Breed at Westminster.

The Morses imported a bitch called Nightmare from Martin Palfrey in 1909; she was in whelp to John O'Dreams, and had a litter of nine – four dogs and five bitches – all of whom were kept for the breeding programme. From this litter, Midnight and Slumber were the only two to be campaigned extensively, and both did extremely well at Westminster. Midnight was Winners Dog in 1912, 1914 and 1917, while Slumber was Winners Bitch in 1912, 1913, 1916, and 1917; both obtained their titles in 1912. Slumber was only defeated by one other Old English Sheepdog throughout her entire show career, by her kennel-mate Ch Brentwood Hero. In 1914 she went Best of Breed and over all the other breeds at Westminster. Another from the kennel, Ominous, went Winners Bitch, and her litter brother, Midnight, was Winners Dog; these two were Best Brace in Show, and together with Slumber they went Best Team in Show. At the 1914 Show, when the number of exhibits totalled 1,721, Slumber went Best in Show and was the first Bobtail ever to take this top award. The judge was the foremost English all-breeds authority Midgely Marsden, thought to be one of the most knowledgeable authorities on pure-bred dogs on both sides of the Atlantic in those days. He stated that in his opinion Slumber was the greatest Old English Sheepdog that had ever lived, and that he had never seen a dog of any breed who more closely resembled its Breed Standard.

Following the death of Mrs Tyler Morse in 1915, her husband continued the kennel for a while, but by 1920 it had practically come to an end. He was an officer of the Old English Sheepdog Club of America, and served on the Board of Directors of the American Kennel Club for many years. A respected judge of the Bobtail and many other breeds, he was one of those responsible for selecting Best in Breed at Westminster in 1926, and as a Group Judge he awarded the Working Group to Mrs Lewis Roesler (later Renner) with her imported bitch Downderry Voyager, at the Westbury KA show in 1929.

Throughout the years, attention has always been focused on those who have done well at the Westminster Show, which as previously mentioned is to Americans the equivalent (although more splendidly spectacular) of our British Cruft's. After the great wins of Slumber, other bitches came to the fore, notably Ch May Morn Weather in 1921 when she got Best of Breed. Other bitches taking this coveted award were Ch Kinnelon Hallowe'en in 1923, Avoca Snowbound in 1924, Ch Donna of Cliffwold in 1925, Ch Lassie of the Farm in 1929, and Ch Mistress Patience of Pastorale (owned by Mrs Renner) in 1935; this was the last time a bitch took Best of Breed. Mrs Renner owned the greatest number of Bobtails to take Best of Breed at Westminster, and her four winners, Ch Downderry Irresistible, Ch Mistress Patience of Pastorale, Ch Downderry Volunteer and Ch Merriedip Master Pantaloons, can be credited with topping the breed in 1933, 1935, 1936, 1939, 1940 and 1942. Mr and Mrs Van Rensselaer have had most Best of

Breeds at Westminster, although not with different dogs; their Fezziwig Kennels won seven Best of Breeds in 1960, 1962, 1963 and 1964 with Ch Fezziwig Ceiling Zero, and in 1965, 1966 and 1967 with Ch Fezziwig Raggedy Andy. In America there is a highly organized system of professional handlers, and I have heard that it is virtually the only way for an unknown person with a good specimen to get the dog to its title, therefore the fact that some owners have personally handled their exhibits to big wins is especially commendable. One name that comes to mind is Mrs Mona Kucker Berkowitz, who handled her Ch Merriedip Duke George to Best of Breed at Westminster in 1959, winning for the third successive year. Although the imported dogs dominated the show scene in the early days, the last time that an import won the breed was in 1938 when Mr L. Collins of Toronto, Canada, won with Ch Ideal Weather.

There have been some famous father/son wins of Best of Breed at Westminster, notably Ch Downderry Volunteer who was the sire of Ch Merriedip Master Pantaloons, and Ch Fezziwig Ceiling Zero who was the sire of Ch Rivermist Dan Patch; the latter, in addition to going Best of Breed in 1968, was also Group 2. Some dogs can be accredited with more than one Best of Breed winner in their progeny. For example, Ch Kennelon Tower was the sire of both Ch Cliffwold Sweet William and Ch Cliffwold Minstrel Boy, Tenet Spook sired Canadian Chs Snowman and Snowflake, Ch Merrie Dip of Pastorale was the sire of Chs Merriedip Bob-A-Long, Kings Messenger and Black Baron, while Ch Farléydene Bartholomew sired Chs Fezziwig Ceiling Zero and Fezziwig Raggedy Andy. There are not so many bitches who can claim to have been the parent of a Best of Breed Winner as well as having attained this distinction themselves, but one which comes to mind is Ch Donna of Cliffwold; she was Best of Breed herself in 1925, and was the dam of Chs Cliffwold Sweet William and Cliffwold Minstrel Boy who were Best of Breed in 1927 and 1928 respectively. Working Group wins came the way of Canadian Ch Snowman in 1932, Canadian Ch Snowflake in 1934, Ch Merriedip Master Pantaloons in 1942, Ch Fezziwig Raggedy

Andy in 1966 and 1967, Ch Prince Andrew of Sherline in 1969, Ch Sir Lancelot of Barvan in 1975 (who then went BIS). 1978 saw Ch Loyalblu Hendihap as Group Winner.

In recent times some very good stock has crossed the Atlantic to become, first, famous in the American show ring and, later, renowned for their progeny. Just about the most famous dog in post-war years was American and Canadian Ch Farleydene Bartholomew, bred by Mr G. Gooch of Kent. Born in 1954, 'Barty' crossed to America at the age of twenty-two months to join the Van Rensselaers' kennel, where he swept to both his titles, had wins at Group level and a Canadian Best in Show, and was never defeated in classes. He began stud work at three years, and though he sired only thirteen litters his name is still very dominant in the breed today, both in America and now in Europe where he figures some generations back in the pedigrees of the Shaggy Wonder Kennel. His sons, Ch Fezziwig Ceiling Zero and Ch Fezziwig Raggedy Andy, were also top winners. Yet another famous son was Ch Fezziwig Sir Basil, so it is quite obvious what a tremendous impact this English import made on American blood-lines.

Another dog which made his mark in America as a stud is Barry Goodman's Unnesta Pim, formerly the property of Caj Haakansson of Scandinavia but now settled in the States. Although a Champion in Scandinavia, Pim won only one Challenge Certificate towards his title in England, and did not leave any progeny behind him when he went to America.

Other well-known exports to America have gone to the Momarv Kennel of Mrs Mona Berkowitz, well respected in this country as a judge of the breed. She had the multiple Group Winner, English and American Ch Prospectblue Rodger, bred by Mrs Lawson. She also brought over Am Ch Shepton Rollingsea Morning Glory, and bought Am Ch Shepton Knotting Prudence from Miss Tilley. Others in California who made purchases from Britain are Dr & Mrs Hugh Jordan and Jim Brown, together with his partner Larry Padgett.

When speaking of imports, the influence of the late Ch Baroness of Duroya cannot be underestimated. She only had one litter but they all took their titles, and it is from these beginnings that the Rivermist Kennel takes its fame. Barry

Goodman has indeed cause to thank the breeder, Mrs Audrey Woodiwiss, for letting him have such a wonderful bitch, who in spite of a sadly early death still left her mark. Ann Lloyd (*née* McGill) sent out Tempest of Dalcroy to the 'Tamara' Smiths in 1963, and he is another whose name figured in many pedigrees. Exported at thirteen months of age, he finished his American title in 1965 when he was just three years old. Another British kennel which made its mark was that of Norman Harrison. His 'Fernville' prefix went all over the world, and has been especially influential in America where he can claim to have bred many Champions.

Scandinavia

Miss Dorothy Malins was pleased that Barnaby of the Embages became a Norwegian, Swedish and International Champion, by Ch Bevere Proud Monarch ex Bess of the Embages, whelped in 1969, and noteworthy in that he pulled a sledge! Also of Miss Malins' breeding was International and Nordic Ch Big Deal of the Embages, who – sent out at 5½ months – had taken his title by the time he was 9½ months old. There are many other famous imports including Norwegian Ch White Mansion Snow Queen, by Ch Rollingsea Snowboots ex Silver Smoke of Oldash; she was born in 1967 and gained her title in 1969. Nordic Ch Raisin of Carrickmines by Top Notch of Tansley ex Shepton Snowball, was born in 1968, imported from Ireland, and gained a title in June 1970. International and Nordic Ch Jolly Bears Johnny, born in 1966 and imported from Denmark, was by International, Nordic and Danish Ch Teddy Bear Bobo out of International Ch Lady MacDuff, and became a Champion at two years of age. Norwegian Ch Unnesta Sebastian, by International Ch Fernville Fair Friday ex International Ch Unnesta Piccolo, born in 1966 and also a Champion at two years of age, was imported into Norway from Sweden.

The first litter born in Norway after the war was from Teddy Bear Bobo and White Mansion Snow Queen, from which four dogs and three bitches were born on 14 January 1969. The second, by Shepton Choice out of Shepton Babette, produced three bitches and one dog on 27 January 1970. The third litter was again out of White Mansion Snow Queen but sired this time by Wrightway Hringdene, and one puppy was born on 14 July 1970. The fourth, out of Lady Shagg by Barnaby of the Embages, produced three bitches and two dogs on 5 August 1970. Fifthly came five dogs and seven bitches born on 23 October 1970 to Unnesta Hurra and sired by Holymans Tarantella. The sixth was out of Poisin of Carrickmines by Wrightway Hringdene, and consisted of four dogs and four bitches born on 31 December 1970. The seventh was out of Lovens Lady by Wrightway Hringdene, and consisted of four bitches born on 5 January 1971. Eighth was another litter of the same breeding, one bitch and two dogs being born on 3 August 1971. The ninth was out of an import from New Zealand whose name is given in my notes as Lady Kiwa of Fraconige; she was mated to Barnaby of the Embages and produced four dogs and two bitches on 1 October 1971. Barnaby also sired the tenth litter out of White Mansion Snow Queen, resulting in five dogs and one bitch born on 14 November 1971. It is splendid that the Norwegian Club is keeping a complete register of the puppies bred. Statistics show that up to the end of 1971 fifty-six puppies were born in Norway, plus eighteen imports from the United Kingdom, one from New Zealand, six from Denmark and about thirty-three from Sweden. Entropion has been encountered, and all stock is being carefully X-rayed. Scrutiny of X-rays is of a very high standard in Scandinavia, and plates which have been passed as clear in other countries have failed the test out there. In some cases, where the purchase of an animal depends on the acceptance of clear X-rays, it may be as well for the vendor to send out plates for inspection by the relevant veterinary authority before the dog is despatched.

In Sweden, a famous dog was International, Nordic and Danish Ch Teddy Bear Bobo, by Ch Unnesta Pim out of Ch Dorothy. He has had many Best in Show wins, and was the sire of numerous Champions. Other well-known English imports into Sweden were Ch Shepton Sally Ann, International Ch Fernville Fair Friday, International and Nordic Ch Rayvil Rowena, Ch Sybilla of Squarefour, Ch Prospectblue Mary

Ann, Prospectblue Angelique, Ch Avenger of Oldash, Inter-
national and Nordic Ch Big Deal of the Embages, Ch
Rollingsea Witchcraft, Int and Scand Ch Rollingsea Honey
Bear, Blueacre Snow Lodge, Prospectblue Tinkerbell, and
Prospectblue Susan. Two of the most famous are a brother and
sister sired by Ch Bevere Proud Monarch: Swedish Ch
Harthacnut and Swedish and Finnish Ch Nancy of the
Embages. In addition, International Ch Reeuwijks Cupid and
International Ch Reeuwijks Charming Girl both came from
Holland, but were originally of British blood-lines. These are
the only names I have been given for listing, but there are
currently more than a thousand Old English Sheepdogs in
Sweden. Quarantine restrictions have been imposed on dogs
from Denmark since February 1970, so there has unfortunately been a complete embargo on all interchanges of
blood etc.

Mention of Finland in the previous paragraph brings to
mind the very successful and go-ahead club there, which was
founded in 1970, can now claim many members, and
publishes its own journal in order to keep its widely scattered
members in touch with each other. One of the best known
Bobtails in Finland was Maid of Kent, bred by Mrs Sylvia
Talbot, sired by Gay Lad of Pickhurst ex Pastelblue Snowlady,
who was born in 1949 and sent to Finland the same year.
Another was the bitch Linnifold Ladyship (by Boldwood
Tangle ex Ch Lovely Souvenir); bred by Mrs A Mason and
exported in 1951, she had several litters by Reeuwijks Festival
King, who was a Dutch import. The dog Blue Prince (by Sir
Milo of Grendonfell ex Jill of the Hills), bred by Mrs P. Davies,
was also exported in 1951, and the dog Linnifold Minstrel (by
Watchers Bobs Son ex Ch Shepton Lovely Souvenir) was sent
over the following year.

Denmark

The Old English Sheepdog Club in Denmark have worked
hard for the breed, ensuring that only the best stock is bred
from, thus upgrading the quality of the breed to a very high

level. With few importations, the type to be observed at their shows is most commendable and of very even standard. I would not hesitate to say I think that their overall quality is perhaps amongst the highest in the world!

Holland

In Holland, the strength of the breed has come from the Reeuwijk Kennel of Mrs Backx-Benninck, who first saw an Old English Sheepdog in the late 1940s in Cardiff. His owner gave her the name of the breeder, and so it was that she visited Mr Tilley the following day and bought a bitch with a wall-eye. This first acquisition regrettably died of hard-pad, but, not to be discouraged, Mrs Backx had another Bobtail sent over by air. This was only intended as a pet, and not for showing, but in the autumn she bought Shepton Grey Idol, and some six months later came Perrywood Blue Bonnet.

From these two originated the Reeuwijks Kennel in Holland and the Shaggy Wonder Kennel of Belgium. Mrs Backx had the good fortune to meet the Comtesse de Changy (one-time President of the South Eastern English Sheepdog Club of England), who owned Shepnor Polly of Pickhurst and later bred a litter with Grey Idol which resulted in seven puppies. From Perrywood Blue Bonnet came National and International Ch Reeuwijk's Charming Masterpiece, and later on Reeuwijk's Honest to Goodness, both Best in Show winners. Mrs Backx exported to Sweden the dog Reeuwijk's Cupid, the sire of Unnesta Pim. She has continued to import good English stock through the years, and is often at the ringside at English shows, especially Cruft's, taking notes of the best dogs being shown. Her kennel has benefited from the addition of some stock from the Fernville Kennels, and they in turn have gone on to influence the breed through the import of their own stock to both Scandinavia and America. Mrs Backx has in recent times imported also from America, with some very commendable successes, from the Fezziwig and Ellenglaze kennels.

Belgium

In Belgium, Mrs Mewis De Ryck of the Shaggy Wonder Kennel benefited greatly from the firm foundations of the Reeuwijk Kennel, and went from strength to strength with her breedings. Many of the Bobtails she sent to America became Champions for their owners, and one such bitch which was sent to California gained fame by being mated to an American Champion and now has progeny back in America who have really 'hit the high spots'. International (and later American) Champion Shaggy Wonder Main Attraction was mated to American Ch Rivermist Hornblower, and from the resulting litter a son called Bobtail Acres Shaggy Wonder Snowman went over to Belgium, where he soon gained all possible titles. Having sired some good stock, he was returned to America to his breeders, Jack and Virginia Herlihy. Mrs Mewis was a regular visitor to England, and it was on one of her trips here that she saw and admired the late Somerstreet Chieftain. Unluckily for her, he was not for sale, but in time she had a son of his out of my Fernville Fernando daughter who became Belgian, Dutch, Austrian, International and World Ch Loakespark Brandy Soda. He took the World title in 1973.

It is known that many Bobtails have been sent out to France, Germany and Italy, but details of these dogs seem elusive.

Australia

Australia was a country where the breed had been limited in its breed-lines. The import regulations were very restricting, in that nothing could be imported unless it had come from a rabies-free country or been through a quarantine period of at least six months in such a country. Because of the rabies scare in Great Britain, there was a total ban on Australian imports, therefore the breeders there had to do their best with the limited breeding stock they already had. Consequently, the breeding-out of some faults has been difficult due to the lack of fresh blood to strengthen the lines. The vastness of the country, and the great expense thus entailed in travelling great distances for any desirable stud, made the breed very regional, which is a great pity since there have been Bobtails in Australia since the first arrivals between 1840 and 1870. Ships' manifests referred to them, but the dogs were not individually named; they were black and white, and all of working stock which was quickly assimilated into other breeds with a resultant loss of the pure strain.

The first serious breeder of Old English Sheepdogs in Australia was the late Mr Picking of Frankston, Victoria, who established his 'Frankston' Kennels in the early 1920s, with dogs from the Shepton Kennels. Pre-war kennels were of the 'Kintora' and 'Warrigo' prefixes. The early Bobtails were always working prospects, and it was not until after the war that they became a show proposition, although even then they were few in number. Most of those shown were bred by Mr Picking from his Shepton stock; the two imports Shepton Blue Dragon and Shepton Be Gentle formed his main post-war breeding stock, and from these came both the workers and the show prospects.

As workers with all kinds of stock, Bobtails have been part of the Australian scene for years, and in the early days they were working sheep out on the Black Soil Plains. Crossbred Old English Sheepdogs now work in Tasmania and New Zealand, and are called Smithfields and Beardies respectively.

Mr James Hull's Ch Wallelin Hi Babe CD was the first Old English Sheepdog in Australia to gain an Obedience title in 1953. He was breeding Bobtails in New South Wales for many years under the 'Southgate' prefix, and during this time imported three Sheptons from England, and some others from the 'Jeabor' kennel. He also owned, under lease, New Zealand Ch Amberford Frea. There is no doubt that the Shepton imports have had a great influence on the breed out there over the years. The Frankston breeding was put back to Shepton imports, and one mating was particularly influential, that of Southgate Grey Abbott to Shepton Pauline, which produced the Chandos dogs. Chandos Humphrey CD has had a great influence on dogs in New South Wales and New Zealand.

In recent times there have been some new imports which have given the breed some strength on certain points. Mr H. Hull was the President of the Old English Sheepdog Club in Australia; they had their first Championship Show in October 1971 in Sydney, when the judge was Mr J. Mitchell who had some fifty-five exhibits to inspect. Best in Show was the bitch Patinka Bo Peep, bred by her owner Mrs M. Burke, and sired by the English import Marlay Pipes of Pan ex another import Ch Vanity Fair of Oldash. Looking through the catalogue, it was interesting to see how many different UK blood-lines are already in Australia. Ch Raydor Scotts Pride and Ch Somerstreet Scotts Lady are two which I chose and sent out to Mr Peter Gardner; he emigrated from this country some years ago after having been the previous owner of my Ch Reculver Little Rascal. Then there was Barkaway Shaggy Shoes, Marlay Pipes of Pan, Whitefall Prospectblue Guardsman, Ch Jeabor Bleu Miss, Shepton Jill, Oborne Superius Girl and Ch Vanity Fair of Oldash. Of special note is Border Riever of Tarras, from Andrew Little in Scotland; from this dog's matings to Chandos Polly Perkins forty-one puppies were produced, no less than fifteen of which have become Australian Champions. By going back a generation on two of the imports, I was interested to find that Ch Vanity Fair of Oldash came from the mating of Ch Bevere Proud Monarch and Bridewell Blue Mist, while Shepton Jill (bred by Mr John Wasley) came from the mating of Broadwell National Emblem and Broadwell Bunty. Vanity Fair was born in 1968 and Jill in 1967.

Of late, UK imports have considerably increased, with so many of the currently known UK kennels being represented. Artificial insemination, with sperm from Ch Aberfells Georgy Porgy, was attempted, resulting in the birth of a puppy to an Australian bitch.

New Zealand

This country is fast coming on as a producer of some high quality stock of great soundness, which I was pleased to find when judging in Auckland in late 1978. They have had some new blood, but not on the scale of Australia, which has been used to good effect. Their quality is high, and very even, with some really correct coat textures.

Austria

In common with many other countries, Austria has benefited from the introduction of new blood.

Ireland

A successful partnership in Irish Bobtails is that of Mr Des Manton and his Irish Ch Southview Aristocrat, holder of 21 Green Stars, 17 Best of Breeds and Working Group winner on no less than five occasions. There is now a very active breed club in Northern Ireland, which serves the breed with enthusiasm. They have worked steadily to attain Championship Status, with their first Championship Show held in 1984, and Mrs Christine Barber making the journey from her Spanish home to judge.

9

Some Common Ailments

THE credit for this chapter should go to my very good friends, David Allison, MRCVS, and his wife Sheila, who took my original notes and expanded them into this comprehensive and valuable addition to the book – for which, my sincere thanks.

Despite the care exercised by an owner, there are inevitably times during a Bobtail's life when sickness does occur, and it is important to recognize its onset as soon as possible. In some cases the owner will be able to treat minor ailments himself, but if he is in any doubt the sooner the vet is informed of the situation the better. The Bobtail is basically a working breed and as such is usually very active both mentally and physically. If the dog is listless, then further examination should be made to try to establish the cause of this, as it may be the first sign of illness. Checks should be made on the appetite, type of bowel motion passed, whether the dog has vomited or not, and whether there are any abnormal discharges from eyes, ears, nose and – in the case of a bitch – the vulva. Any increase in thirst should be noted, also increased respiratory rate and/or temperature (see page 151). If any of the above symptoms are shown, then tell the vet who will decide if treatment by him is necessary. The causes of some symptoms are detailed below, as are some causes of lameness.

Accidents

If a dog is involved in an accident, whether on the road or elsewhere, it may be some time before professional help arrives, so be prepared to carry out first aid yourself. Always remember that after any accident the reactions of the most placid dog may be completely out of character due to pain or shock, so it may be necessary to tie a tape around the nose to prevent it from biting its helpers – a lady's stocking or gentleman's tie will suffice. Try to keep the dog quiet and prevent too many spectators from crowding around. If the dog is very shocked, or you suspect a fractured limb, then place it on a flat board or coat to facilitate movement to shelter.

If a wound has been sustained and is bleeding excessively, then apply a clean dry bandage over the bleeding part – a clean handkerchief will do. If the wound is on a limb, then a really tight bandage may be needed to control the bleeding – this is especially valuable for a cut pad. Apart from these measures, I do not favour any further action on the owner's part.

Anal glands

These are situated at either side of the exit from the bowels, and they give out a lubricating fluid in small quantities when a dog is passing a motion. Should the exit from these glands become blocked, or the glands fall into disuse due to the passage of too soft a motion, the fluid inside them may become semi-solidified, and thus be the start of an abscess. When a dog slides or rubs its rear end on the floor, this is not normally a sign of worms, but of irritation of the anal glands, so it is as well that they are checked then, before the trouble develops into an abscess. Your vet will usually squeeze out the glands, and thus alleviate the symptoms. If an abscess does form, do not interfere with it, but seek professional help immediately.

Canker

This can be avoided if you inspect the ears frequently. In a long-coated breed extra special care must be taken to ensure that the ear opening is not clogged up with an accumulation of hair. The first sign that all is not well may be increased sensitivity around the area of the ears, and you may also notice the characteristic sour smell that goes with canker. A dog which is forever trying to rub its ears against furniture, or one which flinches when the ears are touched, should be very carefully checked. If you do find signs of trouble in the ears, do not prod around as you can easily cause pain and possibly damage. This is definitely another job for the vet.

Constipation

Bobtails are rarely troubled by constipation; in fact, if anything, they have a tendency to loose bowel movements. Provided that plenty of roughage is given, there should be no need to start dosing with any laxative. Should true constipation occur, then try a dose of human Milk of Magnesia or some other mild laxative, followed by a warm drink and a little gentle exercise. Provided that the Bobtail is fed an intelligent diet, with plenty of clean fresh water readily available, and gets adequate exercise, this trouble should rarely occur.

Deafness

I would recommend that you always test a new puppy's hearing before purchase. I never advise keeping a deaf puppy, since there is so much that it cannot be taught and its life is therefore far from full. If there is any evidence of deafness on either side of a proposed mating, then it should not be considered as a breeding propostion. One of the veterinary colleges has carried out research into deafness, with reference to Bobtails, and we are still hearing of quite a few cases, at home and abroad.

Diarrhoea

The first step to be taken when a dog develops diarrhoea is to withdraw all solid food for a period of twenty-four hours – give instead boiled milk, diluted half and half with water, and to a pint of this add one dessertspoon of glucose and half a teaspoon of salt. If the diarrhoea is accompanied by vomiting, then give the liquid little and often – that is to say, a saucerful every half hour; otherwise, give as much as the dog wants, because the fluid loss in the diarrhoea must be replaced. For the next twenty-four hours give only cereal, milk and eggs, with water available as usual. Return to the normal meat diet gradually, possibly using fish or chicken instead of red meat as a start. All breeders have their own pet remedies, ranging from plain boiled rice to a kaolin mixture readily and cheaply available; you will no doubt formulate your own in time. If the diarrhoea does not respond within twenty-four to forty-eight hours after changing the diet, then contact your vet.

Excessive thirst

If your dog begins to drink water excessively there can be a number of causes including kidney disease, diabetes and metritis (see later section). Certain poisons can also cause excessive thirst. It will save valuable time if you take a sample of the dog's urine to the vet with the dog, in these cases; a fairly small amount in a clean bottle is sufficient. This will enable the vet to test the urine and possibly determine the cause of the excessive thirst from this alone, although further tests may sometimes be necessary.

False pregnancy

Sometimes a bitch will behave abnormally about six to nine weeks after a season, begin to 'mother' toys or other soft objects and produce milk from her mammary glands, although the owner knows she has not been mated. She is experiencing a false pregnancy, which is an upset of the normal reproductive hormone balance following a season. The milk flow can be reduced by cutting down the bitch's food and fluid intake, but if this does not help, or if she seems unduly upset psychologically, then professional help will be needed. Once this has occurred it will happen after every season, and the only permanent cure is to have the bitch spayed – i.e. surgically remove the womb and ovaries. Having a litter after one

season will not prevent a false pregnancy following subsequent seasons.

Hereditary abnormalities

1. *Entropion.* This is a condition whereby the eyelids turn
inwards, and the consequent rubbing of the hair and lashes
against the eyeball causes much irritation and discomfort. The
first signs of trouble in this case are excessive tear production
and irritation of the eye. A minor operation can be performed
to correct this condition, but it must be remembered that even
though the operation is a complete success the dog has still
suffered from a defect which is known to be hereditary.

2. *Hip dysplasia.* This is the name given to an abnormal
development of the bones which form the hip joint, and is the
most common hereditary defect in Bobtails. The hip joint is
basically a ball-and-socket joint – the ball being the head of the
femur, which should fit snugly into the socket which is the
acetabulum. In an abnormal hip, the fit is poor and may be
extremely bad, either because the femoral head is incorrectly
shaped, or because the socket into which it should fit is too
shallow. Very faulty movements of the hind limbs may be sug-
gestive of hip dysplasia, but the diagnosis can only be proved
by X-ray examination.

3. *Hereditary Cataract and Progressive Retinal Atrophy.* These are
two eye conditions, which, sadly, are now being found in
increasing numbers. Very few general practising veterinary
surgeons are able to give a complete diagnosis of these two
conditions and if either is suspected, they may wish to refer
clients to more specialized advice. Any owner who suspects
any deficiency of sight in their dog should seek help as
soon as possible.

*Stock which shows any degree of hereditary defect should not be used for
breeding under any circumstances.*

Inoculations

By giving protection at the right time some of the most
dangerous diseases a dog can contract may be prevented.

These are distemper (which includes hard-pad), virus hepatitis, and the two forms of leptospirosis: canicola disease which affects the kidneys and may leave the dog with permanent kidney damage is one form; the other is commonly called rat jaundice, as the disease is characterized by jaundice and is frequently carried by rats, being passed on in their urine.

In recent times another serious disease has emerged. It is called parvovirus for which inoculations are available. Some dogs build up a resistance quite well, whilst others will not develop immunity to quickly. The only certain test of immunity is by blood testing. Very young and elderly dogs are probably at greatest risk from parvo, which can cause damage to heart and digestive systems in severe cases.

Kennel cough is another virus infection, formerly treated with drops administered up the nose. Now it can be incorporated in the other preventive inoculations. All these diseases can be killers, or leave permanent damage to the health of your dog.

Permanent protection against these diseases consists of injections given from ten weeks of age onwards, although temporary protection may now be given from three weeks of age by a different type of injection. It is usually recommended that booster doses be given annually, particularly at times of increased risk or if the animal is being shown regularly. Your vet will always advise you as to the best form of protection for your dog.

Metritis

A bitch may develop metritis, which is an infection of the womb, after whelping, when she will appear listless, off her food and probably run a temperature. A thick, smelly brown discharge passes from her vulva. Prompt professional attention is vital here, as antibiotic injections will probably be necessary.

A different form of metritis may afflict an elderly bitch who has never produced pups. In these cases the bitch again looks ill, drinks excessively and may be vomiting. She does not necessarily have a vulval discharge, in which case her abdomen will possibly be distended. These cases usually occur around the time of a season or just after it. Although medical treatment can help, the vet usually prefers to remove the womb surgically, sometimes as an emergency operation.

Osteocondritis desecans

This is a condition whereby a knock has injured a small blood vessel feeding a part of the head of the humerus (the shoulder joint being the joint most likely to be affected in large breeds, although other joints may also suffer). When the blood supply is cut off, the part of the gristle covering this area dies, and new gristle grows in underneath causing the old dead section to be rejected. The rejected portion then moves around in the joint, and causes pain and disability in the affected limb. Relief can only be achieved by surgery, when the loose piece(s) are removed. Some authorities believe that a hereditary factor may be involved in this condition, but this has yet to be proved.

Poisons

Many different substances will poison dogs who eat them, apart from those well known to us as poisons. Especially with a puppy around the house, cleaning materials and disinfectants – as well as drugs and medicines – should be safely locked away.

Rat poison is an ever present hazard. If the substance involved is Warfarin, found in many proprietary rodenticides, the first indication of trouble may be unexplained bleeding especially from the dog's gums. This poison takes effect by reducing the clotting ability of the blood, so that rats poisoned by it die from internal haemorrhages. Although a single small dose will not harm a dog, a large dose or a number of smaller doses probably will do so. Emergency treatment is necessary if Warfarin poisoning is diagnosed. Often Vitamin K injections are sufficient but occasionally a blood transfusion is necessary. Other forms of rat poison are now on the market, which are more difficult to diagnose and treat, so be on constant guard in rat-infested areas.

Many different weedkillers are now used in horticulture and agriculture, and also by local authorities along grass verges, etc. Some of these may produce toxic effects in dogs, either through eating or licking the substance direct, or through eating a small animal or bird already poisoned by the substance. Vomiting may follow poisoning of this type, but in most cases strange behaviour or muscular twitching are the usual signs to look for, as the primary effect is upon the nervous system.

Gas and fumes have been known to kill dogs accidentally. Make sure that adequate ventilation is always available in a room containing any form of stove. Gas, oil and solid fuel boilers have all been implicated in this type of accident.

If you suspect that your dog has swallowed something dangerous, then attempting to make him vomit will rarely cause harm. Give the dog a piece of washing soda about the size of a walnut, which should be enough to make an adult Bobtail vomit. Alternatively, a very strong solution of common salt in warm water will achieve the same effect.

Senility

Old age comes slowly for most Bobtails. They seem to be a comparatively long-lived breed, with ages of twelve years and more being recorded. Even if no specific illness overtakes a dog, at a certain age his faculties begin to fail and he slows down in all respects. There comes a time when all his zest for living has gone and life becomes a burden. This time is not difficult to recognize, but is hard for a loving owner to accept. However, it is our duty then to take the responsibility, and to make arrangements for the vet to give him his final injection. Nowadays the actual process of putting a dog to sleep is quick and painless, but your dog – and usually your vet – will appreciate your presence at the end.

Skin diseases

These can be divided into two types: parasitic and non-parasitic. Most of the skin parasites carried by dogs are insects such as fleas, lice, ticks and various species of mites.

Fleas can easily hide amongst the Bobtail's thick coat, and often the only way in which a flea infestation can be recognized is by finding flea dirt in the coat of an itchy dog. This substance looks like little pieces of black soil, but if wetted will turn red, as it is in fact dried blood. Flea powder will not penetrate a Bobtail's coat very easily, and so an insecticidal shampoo is needed to eradicate fleas. Apart from treating the dog, its bedding must also be thoroughly washed at the same time, for it is here that the fleas breed.

Lice are less common, but once picked up are more difficult to eradicate than fleas as they breed on the dog, and their eggs – known as nits – stick firmly to the hairs. Frequent insecticidal baths and much grooming are necessary for their complete removal.

Ticks can be picked up from long grass during the summer months and attach themselves to the skin in order to suck the dog's blood. They vary in size from a pinhead up to more than a quarter of an inch across, according to the amount of blood ingested. If you find one, *never* pull it off, as the mouth parts may be left behind in the skin and cause an infected sore. Instead, use a few drops of methylated spirits or turpentine to drug it, when it will drop off of its own accord.

Harvest mites, which cause intense irritation on the skin, mostly have their effect on the underside of the dog where the coat is thinner. This irritant effect is increased if the insects' bodies are crushed, i.e. by the dog scratching himself. If an inflamed area of skin looks as though it has orange-red powder round it, then look more closely as this 'powder' may well be harvest mites. The one consolation is that they are strictly seasonal, only occurring from July to September. Treatment is once again by insecticidal baths.

Even smaller than the tiny harvest mites are the microscopic mites that burrow into the skin itself and cause mange. Sarcoptic mange usually affects the hairless areas of the dog's belly, inside the thighs and inside the front legs, where very itchy sores are found. Demodectic mange mostly afflicts pups and younger dogs, and may show itself on any part of the body, although the head is most commonly affected. In this disease, hairless patches are found with a slaty-blue and scaly appearance, but these are rarely itchy. Definite diagnosis and treatment of mange should be carried out by the vet.

Of the various diseases a dog can contract, skin diseases are the most likely to be transmitted to humans, so early diagnosis and treatment is important. The majority of the parasitic skin diseases are easily treated by the owner, but it is best to ask for professional advice about non-parasitic skin diseases since the causes of these are so varied and numerous.

Temperature

I do not believe in rushing to take a dog's temperature every so often, but there are times when your vet will request that you keep a regular check on it, so it is as well to know how to proceed with the minimum of discomfort to the dog. You need a blunt-ended clinical thermometer, and it is also as well to have a jar of petroleum jelly handy. The thermometer should be carefully inserted about 1–1½ inches into the back passage (rectum) and held in place for up to a couple of minutes. I always leave it there a little longer than the instructions direct. If you experience any difficulty in inserting the thermometer, smear the tip with a little of the jelly to encourage it to slip in more easily. Whatever happens, do not leave the dog while the thermometer is in place, for fear of it getting broken. If you are by yourself and the dog resists your efforts, fetch help, for it could end in tragedy if you have a struggle which results in broken glass. The normal temperature of a dog is 101.5°F (38.5°C), but this can vary slightly from dog to dog, and fluctuate merely from excitement or hectic exercise.

Worms

Two different kinds of worms are commonly found in dogs – roundworms and tapeworms. Roundworms are white, round, and vary in length from half an inch to about three inches.

They are usually recognized in the motions, but may also be vomited up especially by pups. Many puppies are born with roundworms, and the dosing of pups in the nest should start at an early age, i.e. about four weeks old. My puppies are regularly dosed throughout their growing period at intervals of about two months. When adult, the dogs are dosed twice a year, regardless of whether there are signs of worms or not. It is important that a bitch which has been mated is wormed soon afterwards, as she may be harbouring worms which, if not eliminated, will migrate through her body into the unborn pups in the womb. In this case, as with all other worms, it is advisable to use a preparation supplied by your vet, as these are both kinder to the dog and more effective than patent worm remedies.

Tapeworms are composed of a head and numerous segments. It is the segments that are seen both in the motions and hanging on the hair around the anus when they are white, flattened and about a quarter of an inch long. The head needs to be detached from inside the bowel in order to completely eliminate the worm. A tapeworm dose achieves this, and also helps the passage of the dead worm out in the motion. Again, get the appropriate tablets from the vet, and dose strictly according to his instructions.

There are many times when one calls on the services of the vet, but later on when experience has been gained we are able to deal with many of these minor things ourselves. There is a handy book entitled *First-Aid and Nursing for Your Dog* written by F. Andrew Edgson MRCVS, and Olwen Gwynne-Jones, published by Popular Dogs which could usefully be added to the canine bookshelf.

OES Rescue Scheme

Very sadly, the over-production of the breed has brought about the need to organize the rescue of unwanted and neglected Bobtails. The official scheme, supported and approved by the bona fide breed clubs, has representatives on its management committee from the breed clubs. Way back in 1978, the scheme accounted for the resettling of over 300 dogs, and latest figures indicate that this has risen to well over 1000 per year. An average of 'in excess of 100 per month' is frequently mentioned. This is probably accounted for by a variety of reasons. The recession in the UK must surely be held responsible in the main, whilst the use of Bobtails in the advertising world cannot be absolved from some of the responsibility.

Contributions to the fast depleting funds are always welcome, whether from private sources or organized events such as coffee mornings, dances, Exemption Shows. The national organizing secretary is Mrs Jill Harwood, The Old Farmhouse, High Hameringham, Horncastle, Lincs. *Tel*: Winceby 644.

APPENDICES

KENNEL CLUB BREED REGISTRATIONS SINCE 1944

1944 – 182	1965 – 477
1945 – 205	1966 – 656
1946 – 300	1967 – 951
1947 – 274	1968 – 1307
1948 – 295	1969 – 1806
1949 – 256	1970 – 2343
1950 – 327	1971 – 2896
1951 – 269	1972 – 3188
1952 – 171	1973 – 3976
1953 – 189	1974 – 4921
1954 – 123	1975 – 4640
1955 – 126	****
1956 – 116	1978 – 3454
1957 – 94	1979 – 5731
1958 – 172	1980 – 5367
1959 – 173	1981 – 3940
1960 – 161	1982 – 2807
1961 – 176	1983 – 2364
1962 – 230	1984 – 2050
1963 – 274	1985 – 1958
1964 – 310	

In 1976 the Kennel Club changed their registration system, bringing in the recording of litters born, then their eventual transfer on to the active register after the individual animal had been named. This prevented the continuation of the previous method of listing registrations. However, the system has now been changed again.

BREED CLUBS

Greater London Old English Sheepdog Club: Mrs Pauline Rudd, 43 Kings Road, Biggin Hill, Kent TN16 3NJ

Lancastrian Old English Sheepdog Club: Mr Steve Hall, 282 Gregson Lane, Hoghton, Preston, Lancs

Midland Old English Sheepdog Club: Mrs Carol Powell, 71 Florence Street, Chuckery, Walsall

North Eastern Old English Sheepdog Club: Mrs Sheila Curd, 82 Eastern Way, Darras Hall, Ponteland, Newcastle on Tyne, Tyne and Wear

North Western Old English Sheepdog Club: Mrs Dorothy Brocklesby-Evans, 85 Bentley Road, Doncaster, Yorkshire

Old English Sheepdog Club: Mrs Pauline Barnes, 19 Sherford Road, Greenmeadow, Swindon, Wiltshire

Old English Sheepdog Club of Northern Ireland: Mr Des Manton, 9 St Quentin Avenue, Glengormley, Co Antrim

Old English Sheepdog Club of Scotland: Mr Lew McWilliam, 16 Woodneuk Road, Gartcosh, Glasgow G69 8AJ

Old English Sheepdog Club of Wales: Mrs Gwen Mogford, 'Gwynfa', Pontymason Lane, Rogerstone, Newport, Gwent

South Eastern Old English Sheepdog Club: Mrs June Mursell, 'Botarus', Ford Lane, Trottiscliffe, nr Maidstone, Kent

South Western Old English Sheepdog Club: Mrs W. Hodgson, Skyrack, The Highlands, Painswick, Gloucester

APPENDIX C

POST-WAR CHAMPIONS 1947-85

Year	Name	Sex	Birth	Sire	Dam	Breeder	Owner
1947	Shepton Home Guard	D	11.10.43	Nosey Parker of Pickhurst	Snowwhite of Pickhurst	Mrs Shanks	H. Tilley
1947	Bashurst Sally Ann of Pickhurst	B	6.5.44	Nosey Parker of Pickhurst	Snowwhite of Pickhurst	Mrs Shanks	Mrs P. V. Maidment
1948	Shepton Surf King	D	4.8.46	Boldwood Bombardier	Boldwood Bustle	Mrs Grillett	H. A. & H. A. F. Tilley
1948	Watchers Bobs Son	D	11.1.46	Watchers Warrant	Watchers Grey Dawn	Owner	Miss M. Tucker
1948	Watchers Boulgehall Toby	D	11.1.46	Watchers Warrant	Watchers Grey Dawn	Owner	Miss M. Tucker
1948	Dreamer of Northmarsh	B	6.8.45	Don of Northmarsh	Lady Butcher	Owners	Mr & Mrs Hartland
1948	Shepton Perfect Picture	B	11.10.43	Nosey Parker of Pickhurst	Snowwhite of Pickhurst	Mrs Shanks	H. A. & H. A. F. Tilley
1949	Shepton Sonny Boy of Marlay (formerly Marlay Top Dog)	D	20.9.46	Beau Brigand of Marlay	Comedy Starlight	Mrs H. Booth	Mrs L. Jones, after Miss Tilley

Year	Name	Sex	Date	Sire	Dam	Owner	Breeder
1949	Bashurst Polly Flinders	B	28.6.46	Ch Sir John Marksman	Lady Audrey of Warridge	Owner	Mrs P. V. Maidment
1959	Hillgarth Blue Commander	D	7.6.47	Saffwalden Eskgrove Bushy	Pastelblue Top Notcher	Miss Davidson	Mrs Sheffield, later Mr Brocklesby
1950	Shepton Indomitable	D	5.8.48	Ch Shepton Surf King	Ch Shepton Perfect Picture	H. A. & H. A. F. Tilley	Mr & Mrs Howells
1950	Perrywood Blue Charm	B	8.8.48	Ch Shepton Sonny Boy of Marlay	Perrywood Lady Linda of Yasabel	Mrs L. M. Jones	Mrs W. Randell
1950	Shepton Peggy's Pet	B	18.9.47	Ch Shepton Home Guard	Monarch Sunshine	F. C. Padfield	C. Abbott
1950	Shepton Sincerity	B	4.8.46	Boldwood Bombardier	Boldwood Bustle	Mrs W. Grillett	A. Uttley & Miss E. Hulme
1950	Watchers Shepherdess	B	11.1.46	Watchers Warrant	Watchers Grey Dawn	Owner	Miss Tucker
1951	Perrywood Shepherd Boy	D	8.6.48	Ch Shepton Sonny Boy of Marlay	Lady Diamond of Warridge	Miss C. F. Workman	Mrs McLellan
1951	Gordale Blue Lady	B	10.11.48	Watchers Grey Monarch	Jill of the Hills	Mrs P. Davies	C. J. Stacey
1951	Shepton Lovely Memory	B	5.8.48	Ch Shepton Surf King	Ch Shepton Perfect Picture	H. A. & H. A. F. Tilley	Mrs W. Randell
1951	Boldwood Berengaria	B	18.3.47	The Sword of Pastorale	Boldwood Blossom	R. F. Matthews	Mrs W. Grillett

Year	Name	Sex	Birth	Sire	Dam	Breeder	Owner
1952	Kentish Man	D	4.4.49	Gay Lad of Pickhurst	Pastelblue Showlady	Owner	Mrs S. Talbot
1952	Paul of Squarefour	D	9.11.48	Shepton Brave Boy	Prudence of Squarefour	Owner	Mrs I. C. Nicol
1952	Shepton Prince Charles	D	5.8.48	Ch Shepton Surf King	Ch Shepton Perfect Picture	Owners	H. A. & H. A. F. Tilley
1952	Drybrook Forerunner	B	12.9.50	Drybrook Danny Boy	Duchess of Drybrook	Mr & Mrs Elston	G. Self
1953	Shepton Pearlstone Precious Gem	B	12.4.50	Ch Watchers Bobs Son	Shepton Precious Pearleen	Miss P. M. Peart	H. A. & H. A. F. Tilley
1954	Bridewell Major	D	20.10.51	Ch Shepton Sonny Boy of Marlay	Ch Shepton Lovely Memory	Owner	Mrs W. Randell
1954	Bridewell Likeable Miss	B	20.10.51	Ch Shepton Sonny Boy of Marlay	Ch Shepton Lovely Memory	Owner	Mrs W. Randell
1954	Pastelblue Carol Ann	B	14.1.50	Pastelblue Sir John	Cobbydale Periwinkle	Miss I. Webster	Mr & Mrs A. G. Wilkinson
1954	Perrywood Maid Marion	B	15.6.50	Ch Shepton Sonny Boy of Marlay	Daybreak of Shirehall	Miss D. Castello	Mrs W. Edsforth
1954	Watchers Butterfly	B	15.5.51	Gay Lad of Pickhurst	Watchers Sweetbriar	Miss M. Tucker	Mrs S. Talbot

1955	Beckington Tom Tod	D	13.7.52	Shepton Celebrity	Shepton Charming	Owner	Mrs M. Keith Gibson
1955	Roderick of Squarefour	D	22.11.52	Gordale Grey Guardsman	Priscilla of Squarefour	Owner	Mrs I. Nicol
1955	Reculver Sally Ann	B	22.12.52	Pastelblue Sir John	Fridays Beautiful Dream	Mr & Mrs A. G. Wilkinson	Mrs W. T. Rickards
1956	Shepton Grey Monk	D	27.6.49	Saffwalden Eskgrove Bushy	Pride of Yeldhams	H. Lindsell Clark	A. V. Sharpe
1956	Lady Blue of Grendonfell	B	30.3.51	Sir Milo of Grendonfell	Newlodge Lassie	A. R. King	Mrs I. Cooke
1956	Linnfold Mischief	B	30.9.51	Ch Watchers Bobs Son	Shepton Lovely Souvenir	Mr & Mrs J. S. Mason	Mrs J. R. Gould
1956	Shepton Rowena of Squarefour	B	22.11.52	Gordale Grey Guardsman	Priscilla of Squarefour	Mrs I. C. Nicol	H. A. & H. A. F. Tilley
1957	Perrywood Old Faithful	D	6.9.51	Ch Shepton Sonny Boy of Marlay	Perrywood Lady Mary	Mrs L. M. Jones	Mrs J. McLellan
1957	Perrywood Sonny Boy	D	18.1.52	Prince Willow of Lyneal	Perrywood Sun Bonnet	Mrs L. M. Jones	Mr F. Brocklesby
1957	Reculver Sugar Bush	B	20.12.54	Julian of Bewkes	Ch Pastelblue Carol Ann	Owners	Mr & Mrs A. G. Wilkinson
1957	Talmoras Mary Tudor	B	25.4.55	Ch Kentish Man	Ch Watchers Butterfly	Owner	Mrs S. Talbot

Year	Name	Sex	Birth	Sire	Dam	Breeder	Owner
1958	Oberon of Grendonfell	D	23.7.53	Ch Kentish Man	Ch Lady Blue of Grendonfell	Mrs I. F. Cooke	A. E. Mason
1958	Perrywood Bonny Boy	D	6.9.51	Ch Shepton Sonny Boy of Marlay	Perrywood Lady Mary	Mrs L. M. Jones	Mrs E. D. Hallett
1958	Shepton Field Marshall	D	6.11.55	Shepton Wonder	Pastelblue Pantallettes	Mrs E. Storey	Miss K. Roussell
1958	Beckington Lady of Welbyhouse	B	22.8.55	Shepton Bridewell Brave Brigadier	Shepton Butterfly	H. & R. Houghton	Mrs M. Keith Gibson
1959	Nil						
1960	Fairacres Bosun	D	27.12.55	Fairacres Commander	Ingestre Tiptoes	Mrs E. M. Bloor	Mr A. B. Little
1960	Fernville Fernando	D	14.1.58	Nero of Hardwickings	Shepton Silver Wendy	Mrs B. A. Fox	N. W. R. Harrison
1960	Rosalinda of Squarefour	B	22.11.52	Gordale Grey Guardsman	Priscilla of Squarefour	Owner	Mrs I. C. Nicol
1961	Beanville Silver Count	D	13.10.57	Ch Roderick of Squarefour	Amberford Aclea	Miss V. Keeling	Mrs M. Mottram
1961	Thor of Dalcroy	D	6.9.56	Fairacres Commander	Weirwood Shepherds Joy	Owner	Mrs A. McGill (née Lloyd)

Year	Name	Sex	Date	Sire	Dam	Breeder	Owner
1961	Reculver Penelope Jane	B	6.8.58	Julian of Bewkes	Ch Pastelblue Carol Ann	Mr & Mrs A. G. Wilkinson	Mrs K. A. Hudson
1962	Beanville Silver King	D	13.10.57	Ch Roderick of Squarefour	Amberford Aclea	Miss V. Keeling	Mrs I. C. Nicol
1962	Blue Brigand of Tansley	D	9.3.58	Daphnis Fearless	Silver Bell of Tansley	Mrs E. Goodwin	F. Brocklesby, then J. F. Boleyn
1962	Jane of Knockanlyn	B	10.12.56	Ch Roderick of Squarefour	Pastelblue Silver Jewel	Owner	Mrs J. A. Muirhead
1963	Reculver Christopher Robin	D	22.6.61	Nicefella of Danehurst	Ch Reculver Sugar Bush	Owners	Mr & Mrs A. G. Wilkinson
1963	Fernville Fantasy	B	1.4.61	Ch Fernville Fernando	Fernville Flora	Mrs B. A. Fox	N. W. R. Harrison
1963	Rollingsea Starlight	B	11.6.58	Greystoke Gem	Broadwell Rosy Dawn	J. Wasley	Mrs J. R. Gould
1964	Beckington Fernville Flamingo	D	6.1.62	Ch Fernville Fernando	Fernville Fiona	N. W. R. Harrison	Mrs M. Keith Gibson
1964	Fernville Flanagan	D	12.5.61	Ch Fernville Fernando	Fernville Fascination	N. W. R. Harrison	Mr & Mrs M. Smith
1964	Rollingsea Ringleader	D	9.2.60	Rollingsea Surfrider	Ch Rollingsea Starlight	Mrs J. R. Gould	Mr & Mrs S. E. Fisher
1964	Teddy Boy of Tansley	D	7.8.59	Daphnis Fearless	Miss Pam of Tansley	Mrs E. Goodwin	J. F. Boleyn

Year	Name	Sex	Birth	Sire	Dam	Breeder	Owner
1964	Blue Glamour Girl	B	23.6.58	Newcote William	Sally Blue Mist	Owner	Mrs I. Lawson
1964	Rayvil Rosalinda	B	16.6.59	Nero of Hardwickings	Shepton Silver Wendy	Mrs B. Fox	Mr & Mrs M. Smith
1965	Bevere Proud Monarch	D	15.8.63	Baucottblues Boy	Blue Chiffon	Owner	Mrs E. M. Foster
1965	Prospectblue Bulk	D	8.8.63	Eng & Scand Ch Prospect Shaggy Boy	Farleydene Peggotty	Mrs I. Lawson	J. R. Andrews, then Mrs D. Sly
1965	Bess of Coldharbour	B	25.10.59	Reculver Son of Carol	Sally Blue Mist	Mrs I. Lawson	Mrs B. Tidley
1965	Reculver Little Rascal	B	22.6.61	Nicefella of Danehurst	Ch Reculver Sugar Bush	Mr & Mrs A. G. Wilkinson	Mr P. Gardner, then Mrs Ann Davis
1965	Wrightways Glorious Day	B	22.6.61	Ch Rollingsea Ringleader	Amberford Cwoen	Owner	Mrs M. E. Fisher
1966	Bevere Stalwart	D	29.10.64	Baucottblues Boy	Blue Chiffon	Mrs E. M. Foster	R. J. MacKinnon
1966	Prospect Shaggy Boy	D	10.5.61	Ch Blue Brigand of Tansley	Ch Blue Glamour Girl	Mrs Lawson	Mrs Lawson, then Caj Haakansson
1966	Bluecrest Carousel	B	22.8.61	Reculver Hurley Burly	Shepton Katrina	Owner	Miss G. Scribbins
1966	Bumblebarn Holloways Homespun	B	28.12.63	Farleydene Reculver King Pin	Holloways Penny Dreadful	Mrs J. Innocent	Mrs C. W. Pearce

Year	Name	Sex	Date	Sire	Dam	Breeder	Owner
1966	Boss of Duroya	D	6.3.63	Holloways Royalist of Duroya	Azure Queen of Duroya	Mrs A. Woodiwiss	W. Howarth
1967	Prospectblue Rodger	D	26.10.64	Eng & Scand Ch Prospect Shaggy Boy	Farleydene Peggotty	Mrs I. Lawson	Mrs I. Lawson, then Mrs Berkowitz
1967	Rollingsea Snowboots	D	15.5.65	Rollingsea Surfrider	Ch Rollingsea Starlight	Owner	Mrs J. R. Gould
1967	Barkaway Ambition	B	28.3.66	Ch Bevere Proud Monarch	Fairacres Fair Exchange	Mrs E. M. Bloor	Mr & Mrs R. MacKinnon
1967	Bumblebarn Bluejeans	B	29.10.64	Shepton Holloways Benjamin	Faithful Tramp	Mrs A. Maidment	Mrs C. W. Pearce
1968	Oakhill Peter Pan	D	11.1.66	Ch Bevere Proud Monarch	Beth of Oakhill	Mrs M. Hargreaves	Mr & Mrs R. Ashcroft
1968	Sukray Statesman	D	6.12.64	Ch Fernville Fernando	Prospectblue Haze	R. Stretton	Mr & Mrs Westwell
1968	Prospectblue Cindy	B	26.10.64	Ch Prospect Shaggy Boy	Farleydene Peggotty	Mrs I. Lawson	M. Garnett
1968	Shepton Pick of the Bunch	B	15.2.65	Rusherman	Gittisham Minx	F. Bussell	J. Featherstone
1968	Viento Sceaphirde Rhapsody in Blue	B	17.5.65	Baucottblues Boy	Knotting Silver Rippel	Mrs B. John	Mr & Mrs Wallis
1969	Pendlefold Prince Hal	D	1.8.67	Ch Oakhill Peter Pan	Smokey Jane of Nelson	C. Riddiough	Mr & Mrs C. Riddiough
1969	Wrightway Blue Mantle	D	18.5.66	Eng & Am Ch Prospectblue Rodger	Ch Wrightways Glorious Day	Mr & Mrs S. Fisher	I. Morrison

Year	Name	Sex	Birth	Sire	Dam	Breeder	Owner
1969	Bumblebarn Paddys Pride	B	21.8.66	Ch Rollingsea Snowboots	Ch Bumblebarn Holloways Homespun	Mrs C. W. Pearce	G. Cherry
1969	Farleydene Fezziwig	B	23.12.66	Farleydene Dombey	Fernville Fancesca	G. Gooch	Mesdames Tingle & Masterson
1969	Hyal Pennys Pride	B	20.11.65	Baucottblues Boy	Roycroft Penny	Owner	Mrs M. E. Ince
1969	Prospectblue Twotrees Arrabella	B	23.11.66	Ch Rollingsea Snowboots	Prospectblue Louise	Mrs G. Little	Mrs I. Lawson
1970	Shepton Happy Go Lucky	D	18.8.66	Baucottblues Boy	Faithful Tramp	Mrs Maidment	Mrs J. M. Shuard
1970	Wrightways Charmaine	B	18.5.66	Eng & Am Ch Prospectblue Rodger	Ch Wrightways Glorious Day	Owners	Mr & Mrs S. Fisher
1970	Gwehelog Welsh Maid	B	2.9.67	Gwehelog Welsh Tammie	Gwehelog Welsh Melody	Owner	Mrs M. Tidley
1971	Twotrees Break O'Day	B	14.5.67	Am & Eng Ch Prospectblue Rodger	Rollingsea Sunbeam	A. W. Little	James Lynn
1971	Rollingsea Twotrees Aurora	B	23.11.66	Ch Rollingsea Snowboots	Prospectblue Louise	Mrs G. Little	Mrs J. Gould
1971	Barnolby Mr Barrymore	D	20.9.68	Ch Oakhill Peter Pan	Barnolby Eastertide	Owners	Mr & Mrs R. Ashcroft

Year	Name	Sex	Date	Sire	Dam	Owner	Breeder
1971	Bumblebarn Ragamuffin	B	25.3.69	Somerstreet Chieftain	Ch Bumblebarn Holloways Homespun	Owner	Mrs C. W. Pearce
1971	Pendlefold Sweet Charity of Cinderwood	B	18.7.69	Ch Oakhill Peter Pan	Smokey Jane of Nelson	Mr C. Riddiough	Messrs M. Banks & H. Bentley
1972	Lameda Pandora Blossom	B	18.10.67	Bruce Faithful Master	Amanda Faithful Lady	K. Rallison	Messrs J. P. Smith & S. J. Mallard
1972	Tynycoed Ty Gwyn	D	18.1.70	Wenallt Masked Man	Beckington Blue Rhapsody	Mrs J. Real	Mr W. S. Real
1972	Nan of the Embages	B	14.7.65	Ch Reculver Christopher Robin	Bess of the Embages	Owner	Miss D. E. A. Malins
1972	Hyal Pastimes Panspal	D	12.6.70	Ch Oakhill Peter Pan	Hyal Pennys Pastime	Owner	Mrs M. E. Ince
1972	Shaggyshire Bumblebarn Caesar	D	. 25.3.69	Somerstreet Chieftain	Ch Bumblebarn Holloways Homespun	Mrs C. W. Pearce	Mrs M. B. Fisher
1972	Cornelia of Trimtora	B	25.9.69	Fairacres Rollalong	Tina of Trimtora	Mr & Mrs R. Marriott	Mrs R. Wilkinson
1972	Mosscarr River Girl	B	21.12.67	Ch Boss of Duroya	Sheba of Mosscarr	Mrs L. Ingham	Mr & Miss D. Brocklesby
1972	Barkaway Tattie Bogal	D	27.11.67	Ch Bevere Stalwart	Brownswall Annabella	Mr King	Mr & Mrs K. L. E. Davis

Year	Name	Sex	Birth	Sire	Dam	Breeder	Owner
1972	Fernville Lord Digby	D	1.7.70	Fernville Raydor Blue Boy	Fernville Merry Widow	Owner	N. W. R. Harrison
1972	Barnolby Snowdrift	B	9.3.69	Ch Oakhill Peter Pan	Marlay Shepherds Song	Mr & Mrs R. Ashcroft	Mrs G. Chambers
1972	Snowserf Lancer of Barnolby	D	20.7.69	Ch Oakhill Peter Pan	Miss Bruin of Halsall	Mr & Mrs R. Ashcroft	Mr & Mrs D. C. Bloomfield
1973	Lameda Lucy Locket	B	10.9.70	Ch Wrightway Blue Mantle	Lena of Lingar	Mr T. Pettitt	Messrs. J. P. Smith & S. J. Mallard
1973	Silverstone of Abbeywood	D	12.1.70	Oakhill Thundercloud	Old Tyme of Halsall	Miss M. E. Dawson	Mr & Mrs H. Smellie
1973	Twotrees Loakespark Tosca	B	19.8.68	Somerstreet Chieftain	Fernville Debutante	Mrs Ann Davis	Mrs G. E. Little
1973	Rollingsea Viceroy	D	4.8.69	Rollingsea Hawthorn Pride	Ch Rollingsea Twotrees Aurora	Owner	Mrs J. Gould
1973	Lomax of Lingar	D	17.11.69	Ch Barnolby Mr Barrymore	Blue Mist of Ramnee	Mr G. P. Mitchell	Miss N. Fielding
1973	Barnolby Wendy Bruin	B	17.8.70	Ch Oakhill Peter Pan	Miss Bruin of Halsall	Owners	Mr & Mrs R. Ashcroft
1973	Rollingsea Venus	B	4.8.69	Rollingsea Hawthorn Pride	Ch Rollingsea Twotrees Aurora	Owner	Mrs J. Gould

Year	Name	Sex	Date	Sire	Dam	Breeder	Owner
1973	Summers Grace of Dalcroy	B	29.7.70	Raydor Bundle	Pandora of Dalcroy	Owner	Mrs A. McGill
1973	Lameda Pearly Princess	B	14.10.70	Ch Pendlefold Prince Hal	Lameda Pearly Queen	Owners	Messrs J. P. Smith & S. J. Mallard
1974	Paddington Bear of Gower	D	13.10.71	Gwehelog Welsh Tammie	Mistyblue Lady	Mrs C. A. Walkey	Mrs G. Chambers
1974	Roncott Blue Belle	B	9.2.71	Dougal Cosy Corner	Jolliver Prudence	Miss R. L. Norcott	Miss S. McCartney
1974	Bluwalder Lady Syringa	B	10.9.71	Champion Wrightway Blue Mantle	Tzandora Easter Bee	Owner	Mrs W. Farrer
1974	Wenallt Trooper	D	5.6.69	Wenallt Farmers Boy	Arabella of the Embages	Owner	Mrs P. M. Jones
1974	Aberfells Georgy Porgy	D	3.5.72	Barnolby Midwinter	Aberfells Cindy Lou	Mrs J. McCunnall	Mrs S. Curd
1974	Whitevale Christmas Knight	D	16.12.71	Master of Chadsley	Blumark Bluelens	Mr & Mrs W. H. Chadwick	Mr & Mrs D. Kilpatrick
1974	Lameda Perfect Pal	D	4.8.69	Somerstreet Chieftain	Bobbycroft Majestic Moonbeam	G. Maidment	Messrs J. P. Smith & S. J. Mallard
1975	Meadowblue Homeward Bound	D	5.7.71	Barnolby Present Hope	Meadowblue Nancy	Mrs M. Meades	Mesdames White & Evans
1975	Lameda Midnight Rebel	B	9.7.72	Lameda Mr Kipps	Andrews Delight	Messrs Smith & Mallard	Messrs J. P. Smith & S. J. Mallard & Mr & Mrs D. J. Moir

Year	Name	Sex	Birth	Sire	Dam	Breeder	Owner
1975	Pockethall New Shoes	D	31.10.72	Ch Shaggyshire Bumblebarn Caesar	Ch Cornelia of Trimtora	Owner	Mrs R. Wilkinson
1975	Beowulf Silver Fizz	B	21.6.71	Barnolby Present Hope	Mosscarrs Morning Mist	Mr & Mrs P. Cooper	Mrs M. C. Hodgson
1975	Tynycoed Pen-y-Bryn of Southview	D	18.12.72	Ch Pendlefold Prince Hal	Tynycoed Merch Dda	Mrs J. Real	Mr & Mrs R. A. R. Cowie
1975	Follyfoot of Shepton and Longdorham	B	4.12.72	Wonder Boy of Shepton	Arabella of The Embages	Mrs P. M. Jones	Mrs M. & Miss S. Duffin
1975	Fernville Special Style of Trushayp	D	22.5.73	Ch Fernville Lord Digby	Fernville Gypsy Madonna	N. W. R. Harrison	Mr & Mrs M. Lewis
1975	Little Princess Pearl	B	3.9.72	Shepton Martini	Oborne Silver Lake	J. Ham	Mrs L. Cross
1975	Bumblebarn New Penny	B	2.4.71	Ch Lameda Perfect Pal	Ch Bumblebarn Blue Jeans	Mrs C. Pearce	Mr & Mrs P. Cooper
1976	Ginnsdale Stargazer Blue of Barnolby	D	19.10.72	Jason Marcos Ginn Junior	Saucy Paw Sheba	Mrs S. F. Ginns	Mr & Mrs R. Ashcroft
1976	Mr Bluedan of the Embages	D	28.9.73	Foxtwist Mr Jumbo	Blueberry of the Embages	Miss D. Malins	Mr & Mrs F. A. Hartland
1976	Arlils Cilla of Southview	B	2.9.72	Ch Meadowblue Homeward Bound	Arlils May Blossom	Mesdames White and Evans	Mr & Mrs R. A. R. Cowie

Year	Name	Sex	Date	Sire	Dam	Owner	Breeder
1976	Tynycoed Merch Lisi Fisi	B	9.10.73	Ch Dorianblue Shepherd Boy	Baucottblues Busy Lizzie	Owner	Mrs J. Real
1976	Sincerity of Barnolby	B	21.4.73	Barnolby Midwinter	Barnolby My Honey	Mr & Mrs J. Hammersley	Mr & Mrs R. Ashcroft
1976	Wenallt Emerald	B	29.12.72	Ch Wenallt Trooper	Twotrees Esmeralda	Mrs P. M. Jones	Mr & Mrs C. Underwood
1976	Rollingsea Christobelle	B	18.12.73	Ch Rollingsea Viceroy	Ch Rollingsea Venus	Owner	Mrs J. Gould
1977	Bartines Most Happy Fella of Jenards	D	12.10.74	Ch Fernville Lord Digby	Bartines Precious Holly	Mrs C. Siddall	Mr & Mrs R. Baker
1977	Sensation of Shepton	D	27.8.73	Kinlochmore Buster	Shepton Miss Rascal	Mrs H. Jones	Miss F. Tilley
1977	Wenallt Andrew	D	13.8.73	Ch Oakhill Peter Pan	Wenallt Wensday	Owner	Mrs P. M. Jones
1977	Cinderwood by Jupiter of Craigsea	D	22.9.73	Ch Lomax of Lingar	Barnolby Cinderella	Messrs Banks & Bentley	Mr & Mrs A. Horner
1977	Cinderwood Great Gatsby of Bartine	D	16.8.74	Ch Aberfells Georgy Porgy	Ch Pendlefold Sweet Charity of Cinderwood	Messrs Banks & Bentley	Mrs C. D. Siddall
1977	Morgans Lady of Amethyst	B	3.10.73	Bobbingay Plainsman of Amblegait	Mosscarr's Silver Lace	P. Kelsey	Mrs P. Tomes
1977	Krisina Magic Moments in Jedforest	B	5.11.74	Ch Barkaway Tattie Bogal	Krisina Miss Jessie	Mr & Mrs C. Underwood	Mrs J. Collins

Year	Name	Sex	Birth	Sire	Dam	Breeder	Owner
1977	Pockethall Shoeshine of Southview	B	6.11.74	Ch Pendlefold Prince Hal	Ch Cornelia of Trimtora	Mrs R. Wilkinson	Mr & Mrs R. A. R. Cowie
1977	Pockethall Silver Shoes	B	6.11.74	Ch Pendlefold Prince Hal	Ch Cornelia of Trimtora	Owner	Mrs R. Wilkinson
1977	Tynycoed Bore O'Wanwyn	B	8.4.74	Eng & Am Ch Tynycoed Ty Gwyn	Tynycoed Mair Fach	Mrs Parker	Mr & Mrs G. Swanson
1978	Monoval Legion Knight	D	14.11.71	Eng & Am Ch Tynycoed Ty Gwyn	Somerstreet Charmer	Owners	Mrs R. and Miss J. Rampton
1978	Pockethall Blue Cloud	D	6.11.74	Ch Pendlefold Prince Hal	Ch Cornelia of Trimtora	Mrs R. Wilkinson	Mr & Mrs R. Wilkinson
1978	Winstonholme Memorys of Oldoak	B	17.8.74	Ch Lomax of Lingar	Drakeshead Redscare Lady Jayne	Miss N. Fielding (Mrs N. Dower)	Mrs D. Oakes
1978	Southview Society Miss	B	6.5.75	Ch Tynycoed Pen y Bryn of Southview	Tynycoed Llygad y Dydd	Owners	Mr & Mrs R. Cowie
1978	Barnolby White Bear	B	27.2.74	Ch Aberfells Georgy Porgy	Barnolby Wendy Bruin	Owners	Mr & Mrs R. Ashcroft
1978	Wishful of Pockethall	B	21.7.74	Pockethall Shenandoah	Fell Gay Lady	F. Austin	Mrs R. Wilkinson
1978	Tagalong Overshadowin	B	22.9.75	Wildahar Lynces Blue Diamond	Hightop Misty	Owner	Mrs J. Eades

Year	Name	Sex	Date	Sire	Dam	Breeder	Owner
1978	Melody of Fairacres	B	14.1.76	Ch Pockethall New Shoes	Fairacres Blue Belle	Mrs P. Guest	Mrs E. M. Bloor
1978	Brithdirs Lady Burry	B	11.12.72	Lynces Blue Monarch	Peggotty of the Embages	D. W. H. Little	Mrs J. M. Woodford (then Mrs G. Mogford)
1979	Trushayp Special Edition	D	21.1.76	Ch Fernville Special Style of Trushayp	Shepshaven Lady Amber	Owners	Mr & Mrs M. Lewis
1979	Branduin Cotton Picker	D	28.5.76	Ch Aberfells Georgy Porgy	Sireva Blue Beauty of Branduin	Owners	Mr & Mrs J. C. Hodgson
1979	Snowfall Gentle Ben of Marleigh	D	27.7.75	Ch Aberfells Georgy Porgy	Waterhead Lady Sarah	Mrs P. Freeman	Mrs M. Fraser
1979	Splendael Sunday Best	D	23.11.75	Ch Pockethall New Shoes	Underhill Lady Jane	Owners	Mr & Mrs D. W. Fletcher
1979	Keyingham Double Daisy	B	20.3.77	Ch Ginnsdale Stargazer Blue of Barnolby	Halsall Brooklyn at Keyingham	Owners	Mrs M. Park
1979	Jemsue Just Jessica	B	5.4.76	Ch Pockethall New Shoes	Arjems Lady Molly	Owners	Mr & Mrs J. Swatkins
1979	Lady Milly of Lamacres	B	29.7.75	Ch Snowserf Lancer of Barnolby	Venator Elixir	Mrs Birkett	Mrs P. Guest
1979	Tinkerbelle of Prospectblue	B	12.5.76	Danum Blue Commander	Blue Morn	Mr Jackson	Mrs I. Lawson
1980	Wizard of Snowserf	D	29.7.75	Ch Snowserf Lancer of Barnolby	Venator Elixir	Mrs B. Birkett	Mr & Mrs D. Bloomfield

Year	Name	Sex	Birth	Sire	Dam	Breeder	Owner
1980	Southview Artful Dodger of Diladue	D	24.5.76	Ch Tynycoed Pen-y-Bryn of Southview	Ch Arlis Cilla of Southview	Mr & Mrs R. Cowie	Mr R. McNamara
1980	Beauville Whoops a Daisy	B	21.6.76	Ch Ginnsdale Stargazer Blue of Barnolby	Trunulla Midsummers Dream	Owner	R. Hutchinson
1980	Longdorhams Sheps Folly	D	5.3.77	Ch Dorianblue Shepherd Boy	Ch Follyfoot of Shepton and Longdorham	Owners	Miss S. & Mrs M. Duffin
1980	Bumblebarn Scramble of Pelajilo	B	13.9.75	Ch Aberfells Georgy Porgy	Ch Bumblebarn Ragamuffin	Mrs C. Pearce	Mrs J. Layton
1980	Longdorhams Clowns Folly	B	5.3.77	Ch Dorianblue Shepherd Boy	Ch Follyfoot of Shepton and Longdorham	Owners	Miss S. & Mrs M. Duffin
1980	Tumbletop Trademark of Denimblue	D	22.10.77	Wildahar Lynces Blue Diamond	Tumbletop High Horizon	Mrs A. Harlatt	Mrs G. Chambers
1980	Lamacres Super Girl	B	11.2.76	Ch Pockethall New Shoes	Kelly Winter Wonder	Owner	Mrs P. Guest
1980	Oakfarm Strawberry Fair	B	3.4.76	Dustville Mr Universe	Wisebeck Leading Lady	Owners	Mr & Mrs R. A. Goddard
1980	Something Special of Trushayp	B	9.5.76	Ch Fernville Special Style of Trushayp	Trushayp Premonition of Payleblu	Mr & Mrs Pinder	Mr & Mrs M. Lewis

Year	Name	Sex	Date	Sire	Dam	Breeder	Owner
1981	Southview Eliza Doolittle	B	9.8.77	Ch Ginnsdale Stargazer Blue of Barnolby	Ch Arlils Cilla of Southview	Mr & Mrs R. A. R. Cowie	Mr & Mrs S. Booth
1981	Southview Fly By Night	D	24.8.77	Ch Fernville Special Style of Trushayp	Bennington Wistful Hanna of Southview	Owners	Mr & Mrs R. A. Cowie
1981	Pelajilo Simply Sensational of Viento	B	19.2.78	Ch Aberfells Georgy Porgy	Pelajilo Lady Peggotty	J. Bennett	Mr & Mrs F. E. Wallis
1981	Amblegait Artistic Addition	D	20.9.78	Watchglen Wizard	Barnolby Artistic of Amblegait	Owner	Mr R. Owen
1981	Pelajilo Milly Mistletoe	B	23.11.78	Flockmaster John Barleycorn	Cobbicot Polly Flinders of Flockmaster	Owners	Mr M. & Mrs J. Bennett
1981	Jedforest Don Carlos	D	25.4.79	Ch Bartines Most Happy Fella of Jenards	Shaggyshire Little Mo of Jedforest	Owner	Mrs J. Collins
1981	Tynycoed un Prydferth	B	26.11.78	Tynycoed Coedwig Dean	Tynycoed Merch Lisi Fisi	Owner	Mrs J. Real
1981	Darosfield Knights Templar	D	8.5.78	Ch Pockethall New Shoes	Pockethall Bo Peep of Darosfield	Owners	Mr & Mrs Williamson
1981	Woolwood Isn't She Lovely	B	28.8.78	Pockethall Playboy of Brinkley	Tumbletop Talk About Me	Owners	Mr & Mrs M. Mott
1981	Abbyfax Jungle Rock at Trushayp	D	8.5.77	Ch Fernville Special Style of Trushayp	Snowfax Abby Ambler	R. A. Kirkby	Mesdames Lewis & Hayes

Year	Name	Sex	Birth	Sire	Dam	Breeder	Owner
1981	Southview Honky Tonk	D	22.6.78	Ch Longdorhams Sheps Folly	Tynycoed Llygad y Dydd	Owners	Mr & Mrs R. A. Cowie
1981	Beowulf Bo Peep of Hibray	B	10.10.76	Ch Pockethall New Shoes	Ch Bumblebarn New Penny	Mr & Mrs P. J. Cooper	Miss J. Bradley
1981	Pelajilo Myrtle Milkshake of Monoval	B	4.6.80	Flockmaster John Barleycorn	Cobbicot Polly Flinders of Flockmaster	Mr M. & Mrs J. Bennett	Mrs R. & Miss J. Rampton
1981	Jedforest Queen of the Night	B	27.1.77	Ch Ginnsdale Stargazer Blue of Barnolby	Shaggyshire Little Mo of Jedforest	Mrs J. Collins	Mr R. & Mrs S. Rogers
1982	Jemsue the Judge	D	25.7.78	Ch Pockethall New Shoes	Arjems Lady Molly	Owners	Mr J. & Mrs S. Swatkins
1982	Longdorham Folly Footsteps	D	16.4.80	Ch Pockethall New Shoes	Follyfoot of Shepton and Longdorham	Owners	Miss S. & Mrs M. Duffin
1982	Bellablue Prince Charming	D	13.6.79	Ch Aberfells Georgy Porgy	Bon Accord Joy (Irish Champion)	Owners	S. & G. Keane
1982	Lamacres Ben	D	6.1.79	Ch Pockethall New Shoes	Fairacres Midsummer Melody	Mrs P. Guest	Mr V. & Mrs P. Guest
1982	Lameda Pollyanna	B	15.9.80	Brinkleys Ring Lord of Lameda	Rosie Lee of Lameda	Owners	Messrs J. Smith & G. Carter
1982	Wenallt Western Star	D	21.8.79	Copenacre Billy the Kid	Wenallt Magnolia	Owner	Mrs P. M. Jones

Year	Name	Sex	Date	Sire	Dam	Breeder	Owner
1982	Southview Snowshoes	D	28.9.78	Ch Pockethall New Shoes	Pockethall Shoeshine of Southview	Mr & Mrs R. A. R. Cowie	Mrs V. Walker
1982	Southview Saracen of Nyetimber	D	1.5.79	Ch Aberfells Georgy Porgy	Ch Arlils Cilla of Southview	Mr & Mrs R. A. R. Cowie	Mr J. & Mrs S. Curd
1982	Bradyll Ice Poppett	B	16.6.78	Ch Cinderwood Great Gatsby of Bartine	Flockmaster Bo Peep of Bradyll	Owners	Mr K. & Mrs A. Nelson
1982	Cachet of Krisina	B	9.7.79	Krisina Patrolling Tramp	Issabelindas Lass	Mr & Mrs Price	Mr & Mrs Stinton
1982	Pockethall Ballet Shoes of Brinkley	B	26.12.78	Ch Pockethall New Shoes	Ch Pockethall Silver Shoes	Mrs R. Wilkinson	Mr & Mrs P. Tomes
1982	Lamacres Melody Shoes	B	6.1.79	Ch Pockethall New Shoes	Fairacres Midsummer Melody	Mrs P. Guest	Mr & Mrs V. Guest
1982	Targamar Field Marshall	D	17.9.76	Mercerden Bargain Boy	Somerstreet Bonnie	Mrs M. Hulbert	Mr R. W. Hulbert
1982	Boventor Roseanna	B	10.5.79	Ch Pockethall New Shoes	Boventor Love in a Mist	Mrs P. Mead	Mr & Mrs Elliott
1982	Shapod Roly Poly of Arlils	D	3.4.78	Ch Paddington Bear of Gower	Hyal Happiness	Mrs J. Williams	Mesdames D. White & L. Evans
1982	Barnolby Presentation of Gojolega	B	9.8.77	Ch Ginnsdale Stargazer Blue of Barnolby	Ch Sincerity of Barnolby	Mr & Mrs R. Ashcroft	Mrs M. J. Matthews

Year	Name	Sex	Birth	Sire	Dam	Breeder	Owner
1983	Brinkley Bubbly Blue of Watchglen	B	9.11.79	Ch Pockethall New Shoes	Ch Morgans Lady of Amethyst	Mr & Mrs P. Tomes	Mr & Mrs M. Ramsay
1983	Pockethall Silver Charm	B	22.9.80	Ch Pockethall New Shoes	Ch Pockethall Silver Shoes	Mrs R. Wilkinson	Mr & Mrs R. Wilkinson
1983	Meadowsweet Anastasia	B	9.8.78	Ch Aberfells Georgy Porgy	Meadowsweet Katie Sue	Mr & Mrs Herratt	Mr & Mrs M. J. Robins
1983	Pelajilo Pud'n Pie of Bedivere	B	5.8.77	Ch Aberfells Georgy Porgy	Pelajilo Lady Peggotty	Mrs J. Bennett	Miss R. Inwood & Mr S. Price
1983	Malcro Mischief Maker	B	20.12.77	Ch Cinderwood by Jupiter of Craigsea	Barnolby Summer Breeze of Malcro	Owner	Mr B. M. Croft
1983	Lamacres Laura	B	15.3.81	Ch Tumbletop Trademark of Denimblue	Ch Lamacres Super Girl	Mrs Guest	Mr V. & Mrs P. Guest
1983	Trushayp Eckythump of Jenards	D	21.12.80	Ch Bartines Most Happy Fella of Jenards	Sweet Charlotte of Trushayp	Mr & Mrs M. Lewis	Mr & Mrs R. Baker
1983	Raynham Scaramouch	D	27.6.78	Ch Ginnsdale Stargazer Blue of Barnolby	Rollingsea Tresa	Owner	Mrs J. Joice
1983	Southview Canterbury Belle of Macopa	B	1.12.80	Ch Cinderwood Great Gatsby of Bartine	Ch Pockethall Shoeshine of Southview	Mr & Mrs R. Cowie	Mr & Mrs C. Barnes

Year	Name	Sex	Sire	Dam	Breeder	Owner
1983	Boundalong Blue Heaven at Jymta	B	Pockethall Playboy of Brinkley	Boundalong Beautiful Dream	Mrs C. Sinclair-Day	Mr A. & Mrs J. Crowe
1983	Debdale Personality of Gojolega	D	Ch Ginnsdale Stargazer Blue of Barnolby	Tinkerbell Sally of Debdale	J. W. Bourne	Mrs M. Matthews
1983	Oldash Gift of Freedom	D	Barkwith Cassius of Oldash	Oldash Only Make Believe	Mrs J. Harwood	Mr & Mrs Nowell
1983	Southview Celebrity Miss	B	Ch Southview Fly by Night	Ch Southview Society Miss	Owners	Mr & Mrs R. Cowie
1984	Pockethall Silver Lady of Vildon	B	Ch Pockethall New Shoes	Ch Pockethall Silver Shoes	Mrs R. Wilkinson	Mr D. & Mrs V. Reast
1984	Hibray Rock on Tommy	D	Ch Pockethall New Shoes	Hibray Here Comes Summer	Owners	Mr B. & Mrs P. Bradley
1984	Barnolby Wedding Bells	B	Ch Ginnsdale Stargazer Blue of Barnolby	Barnolby White Bear	Owners	Mr & Mrs R. Ashcroft
1984	Southview Crackerjack	D	Ch Cinderwood Great Gatsby of Bartine	Ch Pockethall Shoeshine of Southview	Owners	Mr & Mrs R. Cowie
1984	Woolwood Mr Magoo	D	Pockethall Playboy of Brinkley	Tumbletop Talk About Me	Owners	Mr & Mrs M. Mott

Year	Name	Sex	Birth	Sire	Dam	Breeder	Owner
1984	Brinkley Beautiful Dreamer of Dervance	B	1.8.81	Pockethall Playboy of Brinkley	Ch Pockethall Ballet Shoes of Brinkley	Mr & Mrs P. Tomes	Mr J. R. W. & Mrs K. J. Derwanz
1984	Blunsdons Starlet Beauty of Bobsoak	B	20.8.80	Edwardian Boy of Tumbletop	Smile Awhile of Braemarc	Mr & Mrs J. Brewin	Mr & Mrs M. B. Field
1984	Oakfarm Wild Basil of Roustabout	D	14.4.80	Pockethall Shoemaker of Oakfarm	Dustville Spinning Jenny	Mrs S. Goddard	Mr & Mrs L. Marriott
1984	Simberdale Henry Higgins	D	18.12.81	Ch Raynham Scaramouch	Ch Southview Eliza Doolitle of Simberdale	Owners	Mr & Mrs S. Booth
1985	Barnolby Troubleshooter of Oldoak	D	30.9.82	Weatherproof of Barnolby	Ch Barnolby Wedding Bells	Mr & Mrs R. Ashcroft	Mrs D. Oakes
1985	Brinkley Ballet Dancer on Heathtop	B	29.9.82	Pockethall Playboy of Brinkley	Ch Pockethall Ballet Shoes	Mr & Mrs P. Tomes	Mrs S. Rogers
1985	Kerjalee Madam Moments	B	5.3.81	Pockethall Playboy of Brinkley	Dame Tristy Spangles of Kerjalee	Mrs P. L. Woodford	Breeder
1985	Lamacres Lancelot	D	15.3.81	Ch Tumbletop Trade mark of Denimblue	Ch Lamacres Super Girl	Mrs P. Guest	Mr & Mrs V. & P. Guest
1985	Lamacres Lucinda	B	10.4.83	Ch Southview Crackerjack	Ch Lamacres Super Girl	Mr & Mrs V. & P. Guest	S. Cartwright & C. Thomas

1985	Little Miss Snowflake	B	10.11.78	Danum Blue Commander	Kellington Snow Princess	Mrs Hall	Mr & Mrs D. Baker
1985	Pelajilo Dan Dare	D	24.7.81	Flockmaster John Barleycorn	Cobbicot Milly Molly Mandy of Pelajilo	Mr & Mrs M. & J. Bennett	Mesdames Bennett & Bushell
1985	Pelajilo Nifty Nancy	B	2.4.83	Ch Pelajilo Dan Dare	Ch Bumblebarn Scramble of Pelajilo	Mrs J. Bennett	Breeder
1985	Trushayp El Cid	D	21.12.80	Ch Bartines Most Happy Fella of Jenards	Sweet Charlotte of Trushayp	Mr & Mrs M. L. Lewis	Mr G. W. Morrall
1985	Trushayp Effervescence of Greyfell	B	21.12.80	as above	as above	as above	Mr & Mrs D. V. Sculthorpe
1985	Tynycoed Caradog ap Tegwch	D	22.3.83	Ch Jedforest Don Carlos	Ch Tynycoed Un Prydferth	Mrs J. Real	Mrs C. M. Cherington
1985	Amblegait Atlantic Conveyor	B	20.5.82	Amblegait Adams Addition	Barnolby Artistic of Amblegait	Mr R. & Mrs G. Owen	P. & S. Franks
1985	Lowcroft Cassandra	B	2.1.82	Lowcroft Likely Lad	Sweet Jasmin of Barnolby	Mrs V. Caswell	Mrs J. Cleary

AMERICAN BREED STANDARD
(reproduced by kind permission of the American Kennel Club)

Skull. Capacious and rather squarely formed, giving plenty of room for brain power. The parts over the eyes should be well arched and the whole well covered with hair. *Jaw.* Fairly long, strong, square and truncated. The top should be well defined to avoid a Deerhound face. (The attention of judges is particularly called to the above properties, as a long, narrow head is a deformity.) *Eyes.* Vary according to the colour of the dog. Very dark preferred, but in the glaucous or blue dogs a pearl, wall-eye or china eye is considered typical. (A light eye is most objectionable.) *Nose.* Always black, large and capacious. *Teeth.* Strong and large, evenly placed and level in position. *Ears.* Medium-sized, and carried flat to side of head, coated moderately.

Legs. The forelegs should be dead straight, with plenty of bone, removing the body a medium height from the ground, without approaching legginess, and well coated all round. *Feet.* Small, round, toes well arched, and pads thick and hard.

Tail. It is preferable that there should be none. Should never, however, exceed 1½ or 2 inches in grown dogs. When not natural-born bobtails, however, puppies should be docked at the first joint from the body, and the operation performed when they are from three to four days old.

Neck and shoulders. The neck should be fairly long, arched gracefully and well coated with hair. The shoulders sloping and narrow at the points, the dog standing lower at the shoulder than at the loin.

Body. Rather short and very compact, ribs well sprung and brisket deep and capacious. *Slabsidedness highly undesirable.* The loin should be very stout and gently arched, while the hind-quarters should be round and muscular and with well-let-down hocks, and the hams densely coated with a thick, long jacket in excess of any other part.

Coat. Profuse, but not so excessive as to give the impression of the dog being overfat, and of a good hard texture; not straight, but shaggy and free from curl.

Quality and texture of coat to be considered above mere profuseness. Softness or flatness of coat to be considered a fault. The under-coat should be a waterproof pile, when not removed by grooming or season.

Color. Any shade of gray, grizzle, blue or blue-merled with or without white markings in reverse. *Any shade of brown or fawn to be considered distinctly objectionable, and not to be encouraged.*

Size. Twenty-two inches and upwards for dogs, and slightly less for bitches. Type, character and symmetry are of the greatest importance and are on no account to be sacrificed to size alone.

General appearance and characteristics. A strong, compact-looking dog of great symmetry, practically the same in measurement from shoulder to stern as in height, absolutely free from legginess or weaselness, very elastic in his gallop, but in walking or trotting he has a characteristic ambling or pacing movement, and his bark should be loud, with a peculiar 'pot-casse' ring in it. Taking him all round, he is a profusely, but not *excessively* coated, thick-set, muscular, able-bodied dog, with a most intelligent expression, free from all Poodle or Deerhound character. *Soundness should be considered of greatest importance.*

Scale of Points

Skull, eyes, ears, teeth, nose, jaw, foreface, neck-shoulders all worth 5 points, total 40.

Body and loins, hindquarters, legs, worth 10 points, making total of 30.

Coat (texture, quality and condition) worth 15 points.

General appearance and movement worth 15 points.

Grand total of 100 points.

As approved October 1953 by the AKC.

BIBLIOGRAPHY

ASH, EDWARD, The New Book of the Dog, 1938.

COMPTON, HERBERT, *The 20th Century Dog. Vol. I. Non-sporting*, 1904.

CROXTON-SMITH, A., *Dogs Since 1900*, 1950.

DAGLEISH, E. FITCH, *Dog Breeding*, 1961.

FLEMING, ABRAHAM, *British Dogs*, 1578.

HERESBATCH, CONRAD (trans. Googe), *Foure Books of Husbandrie*, 1586.

HOPWOOD, AUBREY, *The Old English Sheepdog from Puppyhood to Championship*, 1905.

HUBBARD, CLIFFORD L. B., *Working Dogs of the World*, 1947.

IDSTONE, *The Dog*, 1883.

JOHNS, ROWLAND (ed.), *Our Friends the Old English and Shetland Sheepdogs*, 1935.

LEIGHTON, ROBERT, *The New Book of the Dog*, 1907.

LEIGHTON, ROBERT, *The Complete Book of the Dog*, 1922.

SHAW, VERO, *The Illustrated Book of the Dog*, 1881.

SMYTHE, R. H., MRCVS, *The Dog. Structure and Movement,* 1970.

STONEHENGE, *The Dogs of the British Islands*, 1872.

TILLEY, H. A., *The Old English Sheepdog*, 1937.

TURNER, J. SIDNEY, *The Kennel Encyclopaedia*, 1910.

VESEY-FITZGERALD, B. (ed.), *The Book of the Dog*, 1948.

WIMHURST, C. G. E., *The Book of Working Dogs*, 1967.

Hutchinson's Dog Encyclopaedia. Part 35.

Inherited Abnormalities of Dogs (The Animal Health Trust).

Monthly Bulletins of the Old English Sheepdog Club of America (various).

Natural History of Quadrupeds, 1844.

The Sportsman's Cabinet, or a correct delineation of the Canine Race, 1803.

INDEX